MW00532952

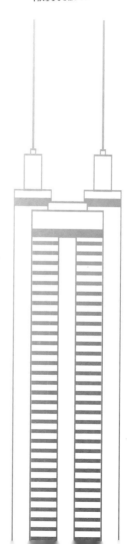

深圳报业集团出版社
SHENZHEN PRESS GROUP PUBLISHING HOUSE

Diwang Sightseeing Building - Credits 韦洪兴

8 MONTHS' WORK, DOZENS of writers, hundreds of interviews, thousands of steps, and an incredible adventure, that's *Shopping in Shenzhen*'s recipe.

As early as we jotted down the plan that later would become the framework of this book, we decided that it should not just be another shopping directory, but a *real* guidebook. That meant: colorful maps, directions and addresses in both English and Chinese, and insightful information. To achieve this goal, we conducted interviews with both Chinese and expatriates and invited them to advise future readers.

What will you find in this book? This guide breaks new grounds by doing something for shoppers that's never been done before: it does not have ads, cuts through the bull and show you exactly "what you need to know."

● **Shopping in Shenzhen** will not only bring you to expatriates' preferred shopping places, but also to places foreigners never dare to go. Rest assured, not that it's dangerous, but rather because of the language barrier; little English is spoken there, if any at all. With our tips you should be able to get around easily even though you're not fluent in Chinese. If you don't speak Mandarin at all, don't panic, jump to Tracy's Chinese Corner page 128 to pick up the keys that will lead you to the best bargains.

● With **Shenzhen's Finest Cuisine** you'll explore Shenzhen's most exotic restaurants. Dreaming of becoming a chef? Give it a try at the world famous Chef Martin Yan's Culinary Art Center.

● Want to stay overnight in Shenzhen? **Shenzhen's Best Hotels** will give you good advice. It not only includes price guides, directions in English and Chinese district by district, and colorful maps, but also reviews by professional travel writers with detailed hotel information and practical tips.

● If you argue that life is not only about shopping, eating and sleeping, we have what you need: **A day in Shenzhen** will take you from your room to Shenzhen's theme parks, art centers, museums and temples, or simply to a peaceful family promenade in one of the numerous Shenzhen's parks.

● What's more? Well, the best is to come. If you thought that Shenzhen was just an industrial city where you'd come and go to do business, a city with nothing much to see, **Splendid Shenzhen** will bowl you over.

I truly hope you will enjoy this Shenzhen City Guide as much as we did writing it.

■ Adriano Lucchese 唐毅德
www.LonelyWriters.com 瓏玲作家

Shopping in Shenzhen

Shopping in Shenzhen	1
Shenzhen Essential	6
Shopping at Luohu Commercial City	8
Dongmen 1001 Shopping Streets	42
Electronics & Women's World at Huaqiang Bei	66
Shopping along the Metro line, and beyond...	96
Furniture and Home Décor	112
Stationery Malls	118
Jewel Shopping Streets	119
Shopping in Zhuhai, Antiques in Zhongshan	120
Shopping in Dongguan, Houjie, and Humen	122
Shenzhen Souvenir line	126
Tracy's Chinese Corner	128

Shenzhen's Finest Cuisine

Shenzhen's Finest Cuisine	146
Chef Martin in Shenzhen	147
The Shenzhen Food Guide	152

(Left margin: 深圳购物 · SHOPPING IN SHENZHEN · www.SZCityGuide.com)

Shenzhen's Best Hotels

Shenzhen's Best Hotels	174
Hotels in Luohu	178
Hotels in Nanshan	180
Hotels in Futian	188
Hotels in Bao'an	191
Hotels in Yantian	192

A Day in Shenzhen

A Day in Shenzhen	196
Getting There	208

Splendid Shenzhen

Splendid Shenzhen	220
General Index	254

Shopping in Shenzhen

Shopping in Shenzhen

深圳 精华	Shenzhen Essential	6
罗湖 商业城	Shopping at Luohu Commercial City	8
东门 老街	Dongmen 1001 Shopping Streets	42
华强北	Electronics & Women's World at Huaqiang Bei	66
地铁站 购物	Shopping along the Metro Line, and beyond...	96
家居	Furniture & Home Décor	112
文具	Stationery Malls	118
珠宝	Jewel Shopping Streets	119
珠海 中山	Shopping in Zhuhai Antiques in Zhongshan	120
东莞 购物	Shopping in Dongguan, Houjie & Humen	122
纪念品	Shenzhen Souvenir Line	126
汉语角	Tracy's Chinese Corner	128

Shopping in Shenzhen, an overview

I T IS SAID that each year millions of shoppers come and go to Shenzhen. The city that was some years ago an industrial area has rapidly developed into a Mecca for shoppers.

Shenzhen has to offer in terms of shopping most of what any big city does, and in some areas, even more.

Even though the city is more and more *foreigner-friendly*, there are still difficulties for foreigners to do shopping in and around Shenzhen.

Where to go? What to buy? How to make myself understood? How to get the best bargain? What bus should I take? What's the nearest Metro station? All are some of the questions we heard hundreds of times while conducting interviews for *Shopping in Shenzhen.*

Here you go. In short, if you want to follow the crowd, head off to Luohu Commercial City 罗湖商业城 (LCC). There is not a single person we met in Shenzhen or Hong Kong that didn't know about LCC. Even though all you can dream is gathered into a single 5-floor building, it is still difficult to find your way around. If you've been there, you know what I mean. To make your experience easier, we have gathered hundreds of tips, organized floor by floor and shop by shop into a single section. We have also laid out colored floor maps with color codes and stall numbers for you to go straight to the designated area. For ultimate experiences, we have also included blank floor maps to jot down your best findings. Don't forget to report them at www.szCityGuide.com!

Here it's becoming more interesting. If you're more adventurous, take the MTR at Luohu Train Station, get off 2 stations later, at Laojie Station - 老街 站. Leave the commercial building via Exit A. You will be soon in the thick of it. This huge place is called Dongmen shopping streets 东门老街. If you are accustomed to LCC and think that's all there is in Shenzhen, you will be greatly surprised. At Dongmen, you see mostly Chinese shoppers. Barely any foreigners dare to go shopping in Dongmen. Why? Probably because there are no maps, no street signs in English and the staff in the shops don't speak English. But consider this: prices are generally lower than in LCC, quality tends to be higher, and there are virtually no touts in Dongmen. Armed with the 3D Dongmen map we drew for you and with Tracy's Chinese Corner section, you should have no problem finding your way around and getting the best bargains. Give it a try!

If you're interested in electronics, head off to Huaqiang Bei 华强北. It's 5 only stations away from LCC. Get off at Huaqiang Lu 华强路 via Exit A, turn left, follow the crowd, go up the escalator and keep going straight. You will soon hit Huaqiang Road 华强路. Look up and you'll see Saige/SEG 塞格, the most famous electronic market and also the highest steel tube concrete buiding in the world.

Want to shop for home décor? Head to the 4 Dragons Home, also called Light Industrial Products district. Hundreds of small individual shops are gathered into 2 large buildings. There, you will find home décor at very reasonable prices. The choice is huge with top quality.

If you have time to venture out of Shenzhen, go to the underground Gongbei Port Plaza 拱北口岸广场 at Zhuhai 珠海, which offers bargains galore in clothes, shoes, handbags and outdoor sporting equipment.

Love antiques? Zhonshan Antique Market 中山华财古玩城 is a place where hundreds of stalls offer beautiful pieces of furniture or objects-d'arts ranging from hand-painted jewelry boxes to large ornate armoires.

If you have heard of places around Shenzhen where you can purchase pieces of furniture, leather goods, and clothes at very low price, then it is undoubtly Dongguan, Houjie and Humen 东莞、厚街，虎门.

When your family or friends ask you to bring a souvenir from Shenzhen what do you say? Well, we've got what you need, check out the brand new Shenzhen Souvenir Line created by the lovely Sheirley.

Ok, now that you've got essential tips, addresses and directions in both English and Chinese, wouldn't it be handy to have a colorful map with all that on it? Check out the Shenzhen Essential map, page 6.

■ Brought to you by
Adriano Lucchese 唐毅德
www.LonelyWriters.com 珑玲作家

Shopping in Shenzhen's **Contents**

Shopping in Shenzhen, an overview	2
Shenzhen Essential	6
Luohu Commercial City	8
Shopping on the 1st Floor	11
Shopping on the 2nd Floor	13
Shopping on the 3rd Floor	15
Shopping on the 4th Floor	19
Shopping on the 5th Floor	23
Luohu Shopping Index	24
The Shenzhen Silk Road Fantasy for Women	26
Write down your own findings	29
Tea World in Luohu	38
Massage in Luohu	40
Dongmen 1001 Shopping Streets	42
Dongmen 3D Shopping map	44
Shopping at Dongmen	46
Fashion	47
Shoes	50
Fabric	54
Arts	58
Shopping Malls	60
Kitchen equipment	63
Staying overnight in Dongmen	64
Huaqiang Bei Area, Electronics & Women's World	66
Huaqiang Bei quick shopping advice table	68
Huaqiang Bei 3D Shopping map	70
Huaqiang Bei Table of Contents	72
Computers & Electronic Components	73
Other Computer Shopping Places	78
2nd hand Computers & Accessories	80
Mobile Phones & Accessories	80
Audio-Video & Electronics	83

深圳购物

SHOPPING IN SHENZHEN

www.szCityGuide.com

深圳购物

Other Products	86
Women & Children at Huaqiang Bei	88
Shopping along the Metro line, and beyond...	96
Shopping in Nanshan	104
Furniture and Home Décor	112
Home Décor	112
Home Furnishings	113
Home Furnishings & DIY	115
Kitchen equipment	116
Stationery Malls	118
Jewel Shopping Streets	119
Shopping in Zhuhai, Antiques in Zhongshan	120
Zhuhai	120
Zhongshan Antique City	120
Shopping in Dongguan, Houjie, and Humen	122
Shenzhen Souvenir line	126
Tracy's Chinese Corner	128
Get your own Chinese Dictionary	145

SHOPPING IN SHENZHEN

WWW.SZCITYGUIDE.com

Shenzhen Essential

Shenzhen comprises 6 districts, Luohu 罗湖区, Futian 福田区, Nanshan 南山区, Bao'an 宝安区, Longgang 龙岗区, and Yiantian 盐田区.

Refer to the map below to locate the most essential shopping places in Shenzhen as well as ferries, airport, key customs, MTR stations in

SHOPPING IN SHENZHEN

www.szCityGuide.com

深圳购物

both Chinese and Pinyin, and some places of interest. Go to **page 125** to locate Macao 澳门, Guangzhou 广州, Shenzhen 深圳, Hong Kong 香港, Hong Kong International Airport 香港国际机场, Zhongshan 中山, Dongguan 东莞, Zhuhai 珠海, and more.

www.szCityGuide.com

Luohu Commercial City

As SOON AS you exit the Chinese Immigration you'll find yourself inside the Luohu Commercial City. The LCC is not an attractive building, rather it is a functional, five-storey complex selling almost everything you could imagine at a fraction of the cost elsewhere. Try to ignore the touts selling DVDs and watches. Starting at the fifth floor with the fabric and tailors is a good idea. If you pick a quiet day it may be possible to schedule a first fitting for later in the same day. Here are two good dim sum restaurants on the fifth floor too. Artworks and embroidery are good buys here.

Massage, haircuts, manicure and pedicure are good ways to relax from the hurly-burly of shopping. Even a basic shampoo & blow dry comes with a head and shoulder massage. All of these services cost a fraction of the price you'd pay in Hong Kong. It is important to bargain hard in Luohu. Frequently the first price mentioned will be 4 times the true value of the goods. Be prepared to walk away if the goods are over-priced but remain polite and always smile. Remember the vendor has to make a living too.

Most day-trippers from Hong Kong do not venture beyond Luohu Commercial City and thus miss out on the atmosphere of Dongmen, where most of the Shenzhen locals shop. The MTR station and bus station are located beneath LCC. Free shuttle buses are available to hotels and spa/massage centres from the underground bus station too.

At Luohu, cash is highly recommended. Some places charge an extra 10% for credit card purchases. The shop assistants will bring you to shops that have credit card processing machines.

■ Introduction by Yolanda Favreau

Luohu Commercial City	罗湖商业广场
✉	Luohu Commercial City, Luohu Train station 罗湖区火车站罗湖商业城
✆	Tel: +86 755 8233 8178
🚌	MTR: Luohu Station - 罗湖站 , Bus: 1, 7, 12, 17
⌛	9:30am - 10pm
🖱	http://www.tosz.com (Chinese)

It's never been easier!

FOR EACH FLOOR use the table in which we have indicated the expats' recommended places to get your best buy:

1. **S**elect the shopping category
2. **G**et the store location and shopping tips
3. **L**ocate the stall using the map on the left page

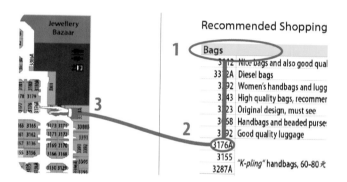

Recommended Shopping

1 Bags

3 12	Nice bags and also good qual
33 2A	Diesel bags
3 92	Women's handbags and lugg
3 43	High quality bags, recommer
3 23	Original design, must see
3 68	Handbags and beaded purse
3 92	Good quality luggage
3176A	
3155	"K-pling" handbags, 60-80 元
3287A	

● Refer to the General Shopping Index at the end of this section to browse through the entire Luohu Commercial City.

● You will also get an **blank** floor map to jot down your **own** best places. Don't forget to register at www.**sz**CityGuide.com and report your findings !

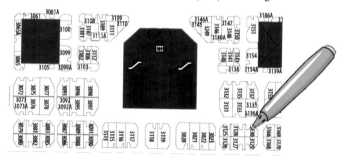

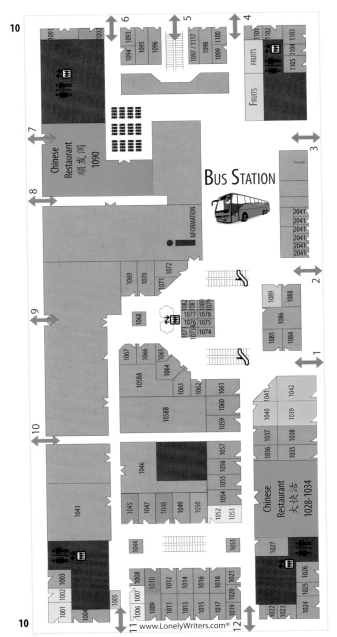

Shopping on the 1st Floor

Arts

1045 1048	Excellent pieces of jade and ceramics statues from Foshan, well designed and reasonable prices
1010	Chinese boxes and calligraphy work. Lots of small little Chinese art pieces
1092	Chinese Ancient Dynasties

Bags

1006 1007	Well designed bags, handbags, clean shops, reasonable prices
1052 1053	Good selection of handbags and bags

Clothes

Blue Jeans & T-shirts

1050 1089	Wide choices of blue jeans & T-shirts

Children's Wear

1089	Wide choice of children's shoes

Restaurants

1090	Chinese Restaurant Shunfage 顺发阁

1028	Chinese Restaurant Dakuaihuo 大快活

Fabric

1039 - 1042	Near Exit 11 is the biggest store in LCC selling curtains, beddings, fabric, quilts, etc. Good quality and reasonable prices. Possibility to have your curtains and beddings designed and made on the spot. Ask the staff to come to your home to take measurement and give you some advise. Grace +86 755 8232 6018, 138 2522 8201

Food

Check out the stores next to 1101 selling fruits, fruit juices, nuts and snacks

Shoes

1005	Shoemaker located next to entrance 11

Toys

1001 1002	Remote controlled toys

Don't forget to register at www.szCityGuide.com to report your findings!

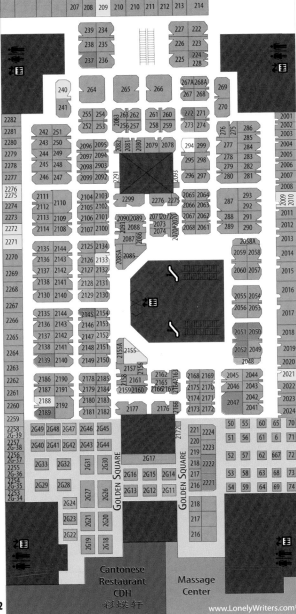

www.LonelyWriters.com®

深圳购物

Shopping on the 2nd Floor

Bags

2010	Computer bags and luggage
240 209	Hand-made handbags, good quality
2276	Large choice of handbags & shoes
2272	Italian leather, good choice & quality, fixed prices
2271	Luggage, travel bags *"Swiss"*
2133	Well designed handbags & shoes
2021	Chinese traditional handbags
2155	Evening handbags
2188	Well designed bags, slightly expensive but good quality

Shoes

Chinese Style Shoes

2048	Large choice of Chinese shoes for adults & babies

Men & Women - All Styles

273 2159	Well designed shoes
2133	Handbags & shoes
2045	*"Crocs"* style shoes
2152	Good quality women shoes

Clothes

Blue Jeans

2050	Large choice of jeans, T-shirts and *"D&G"* clothes

T-Shirts

2139	Well designed and good quality T-shirts
2221	Wide choice of T-shirts

Children's Wear

237	All for children, shoes, T-shirts, socks, pants and some toys
2047	Children's shoes and clothes

Chinese Traditional

298	Chinese traditional jackets
2021	Chinese traditional handbags

Underwear

2222	Wide selection of women underwear

Men's Ties

2139	Wide choice of men's ties

Arts

2160	
2145	Nice pieces of jade
2189	

Beauty

2129	Manicure tool sets

Jewelry

2128	Well designed jewels
2259 2G-39	Best place to purchase all the necessary pieces to do your own necklaces, i.e. thread, pearls, etc.
2G-47	Located at the Golden Square, nice stones, excellent necklaces at about 80元 piece, ask for Weiki
2G-22	G.Square, beautiful necklaces
2G-11 2G-24	G.Square, beautiful pearls

Cashmere & Pashmina

272 224 2051 2052	Good quality cashmere and pashmina

Food

294	Food for diabetic

Restaurants

Cantonese Restaurant CDH
Caijiexuan 彩蝶轩

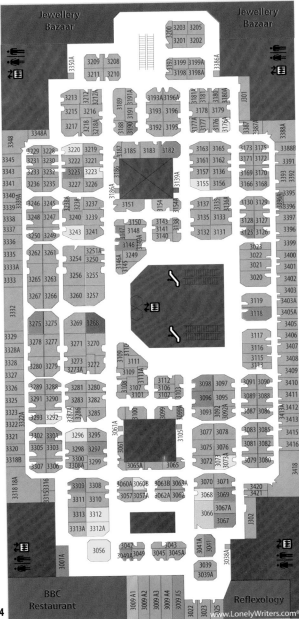

深圳购物

Shopping on the 3ʳᵈ Floor

Bags

3112	Nice bags and good quality leathers
3312A	Diesel bags
3292	Women's handbags and luggage
3243	High quality bags
3223	Original design, must see
3068	Handbags and beaded purses
3192	Good quality luggage
3176A	
3155	"K-pling" handbags, 60-80 元
3287A	
3220	

Shoes

Sport Shoes

3239	Sport shoes and T-shirts. Good quality

Men & Women - All Styles

3095	Good quality shoes and boots
3062	Good quality shoes and men's jackets
3255	Wide choice of good quality shoes at fixed prices
3257	

Men's Shoes

3131	Smart design, good quality leather and finishing

Dancing Shoes

3099A	Specialized in dancing shoes; good quality and prices; check the same at 4035/4F

Clothes

Blue Jeans

3147	Wide selection of blue jeans and T-shirts

Women's Fashion

3182	Fashion design dresses
3118	
3069	Fashion design dresses and coats
3067	
3309	Fashion design women's T-shirts
3190	Fashion design dresses

Underwear

3041	Wide selection of underwear men and women

Outerwear

3049A	"K-way", parkas, outdoor clothing

Children's Wear

3396A	Small stall but wide selection of children's wear
3297	Children's wear, some toys

Chinese Traditional

3146	Chinese dresses, shoes. Highly recommended
3098	
3009 A5	Chinese dresses
3099A	
3125	

Golf

3225	Wide choice of Golf equipment, clothes, shoes. Reasonable prices

Socks

3301	Wide selection at reasonable prices

Curtains & Beddings

3066	Large shop with good selection of beddings, curtains, sofa covers, cushions, table runners, wooden blinds

Eye Glasses

3268	Wide choice of spectacles and sun glasses

Arts

3196	Wide selection of mirrors and frames
3001A	Small metal statuettes
3139A	Zodiacal figurines

Beauty

3009 A1	*OPI* manicure
3313A	Wide range of quality manicure tool sets

Jewelry

3029	Good quality and service. Highly recommended
3282 3154	Cultured pearls from Zhejiang province
3154	Costume jewelry; Cultured pearls from Zhejiang province

Cashmere & Pashmina

3275	Wide selection of pashmina and silk. Good quality.

Restaurants

BBC Restaurant
Western Food

Fabric at Luohu Shopping Center

On the 5th floor of LCC, there is a great selection of fabrics, especially nice are the silks. Initial prices given at this market are higher than at the Dongmen market because a lot of HK shoppers come to Luohu. If you can, make it known that you live in Shenzhen and try to bargain. Often, prices will come down. Most shopkeepers here speak at least a little English. For that reason, shopping here is easier than at Dongmen. Several trim shops are located throughout the market.

Don't forget to register at www.szCityGuide.com
to report your findings!

SHOPPING IN SHENZHEN

www.szCityGuide.com

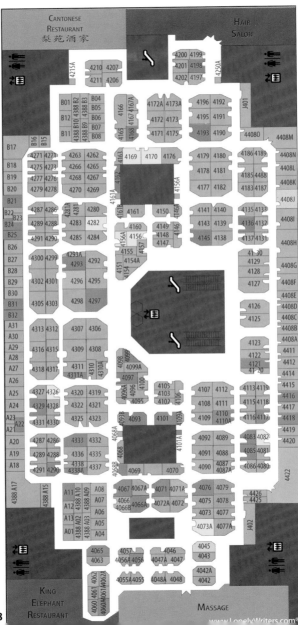

CANTONESE
RESTAURANT
梨苑酒家

HAIR
SALON

KING
ELEPHANT
RESTAURANT

MASSAGE

Shopping on the 4ᵗʰ Floor

Bags

4282	Excellent cosmetics bags
4326	Wide choice of fabric and leather bags
4073A	Luggage, *"Elle"* bags
4156A 4160	Relax & young style bags
4160A	*"K-pling"* , *"Le sport"* sac, *"Agnes B"*
4282	Cosmetics bags
4082	*"Agnes B"* bags
4069	Stylish fashionable designs
4106	Evening bags
4296 4170	Good choice of luggage and backpacks

Belts

4079 4070	Wide selection of good quality belts
4078 4086	Belts, bags and shoes

Shoes

Dancing Shoes

4135	Small stall but wide choice of ballerinas and other dancing shoes

Casual Shoes

4071A	Jogging & city shoes

Men & Women - All Styles

4337 4335	Reasonable prices, large selection of shoes
4197 4388	Good quality shoes
4062	Good quality shoes and large selection of socks

Smart Shoes

4086	Smart style; also sells belts

Clothes

Blue Jeans

4083	Wide choice of blue jeans & Fashionable T-shirts - Jeans ~100 元
4333	Good selection of blue Jeans, T-shirts & jackets. Carries *"Agnes B"* bags
4107	Wide choice of blue jeans & T-shirts
4160	Blue jeans, T-shirts, relax & young style bags
4290	Blue jeans & belts

Women's Fashion

4145	Good choice of fashionable dresses and women's bags
4308	Stalls B-32, B-31, B-24-25 Women's fashion
4416	Women's fashion
4121	Well designed dresses
4197	Women's fashion & shoes
4085	Women's fashion & *"Pink"* shirts
4338A	Women's fashion & well designed T-shirts

Leather

4418 4293 4329	Leather & Fur

Underwear

4065	*"Snowflakes"* underwear
4297	Also caries children's wear
4193	Men & women underwear
4198	Underwear and socks
4136 4162	Women's underwear

Men's Fashion

4160	Jackets, T-shirts & pants

4045	Jackets, blue jeans & T-shirts
4206	Jackets, T-shirts & pants

Also check the Blue Jean section, most of them carry men's fashion

Children's Wear

4110	
4197	
4168	Specialized in children's wear
4068B	
4311A	

Chinese Traditional

4438-B21 4117	These stalls propose Chinese dresses/shirts from various Chinese minorities at reasonable prices. Highly recommended.
4068	Traditional Chinese dresses
4288-A11	Traditional Chinese dresses & Japanese Kimonos

Outerwear

4206	Winter clothes, Ski attire, & *"Tommy Bahama"* shirts

Caps & Hats

4101	Large selection of caps of all kinds and colors

Towels

4388-A22	Low prices, reasonably good quality and wide choice of bath towels

Golf

4388-A03	T-shirts, shoes, clubs, bags, etc. at reasonable prices

Socks

4062	Socks & shoes
4198	Socks & underwear

Household Furnishing

4045	Beddings & tablecloths and runners, reasonable prices
4408J	Wide selection of curtains

4422	Big store next to FuMei massage, selling large range of curtain fabrics

Jewelry

4090	Well designed jewels
4167	Well designed jewels, beautiful pearls
4160 4296	Nice jewels & well-designed hand bags
4066	Wide choice of jewels with fancy design

Arts

4101A	Small stall selling Chinese paper-cut work (opposite 4091), 137 1435 3638
4071	Silver statues and tea pots
4067 4168	Jade artwork
4066A	Crystals & stones
4060A	Nice little statues made of terracotta from Jianxi 江西
4097	Broidery artwork
4093A	Stamp made of jade with name in Chinese characters.
4099	Small 50 元, medium 100 元, big 150 元. Calligraphy work 80 元
4056	Have your portrait made here

Cashmere & Pashmina

4076	Wide choice of cashmere & pashmina, scarf ~100 元
4166	Good selection of cashmere & pashmina

Beauty

4207	*OPI* manicure, manicure 20 元, pedicure 30 元

Restaurants

Liyuan Jiujia Cantonese, 梨苑酒家

King Elephant, Cantonese & Thai Cuisine

深圳购物   SHOPPING IN SHENZHEN   www.szCityGuide.com

Don't forget to register at www.szCityGuide.com
to report your findings!

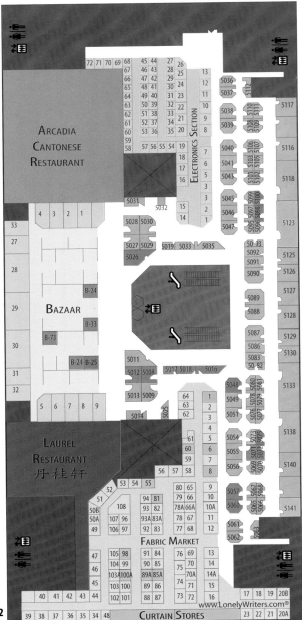

ARCADIA
CANTONESE
RESTAURANT

ELECTRONICS SECTION

BAZAAR

B-24
B-33
B-73
B-24 B-25

LAUREL
RESTAURANT
丹桂轩

FABRIC MARKET

CURTAIN STORES

www.LonelyWriters.com®

Shopping on the 5ᵗʰ Floor

Tailors

5100	English spoken. Suits, pants, shirts, dresses. Ask for Helen 130 7693 2598
5098	Good service and quality
5026	Hong Kong tailor. English spoken. Good quality men suits
5048	Good service and quality
5075	Bring your own material or select it from the store. Possible to have your clothes sent to Hong Kong. 137 1523 0969
5072	English spoken. Ask for Moly. 138 2883 2788
5057	Ask for Jansion. 139 0247 5576
5060A	Possibility to order via Internet at www.larkapparel.com or phone 137 1400 7671. **Recommended by many expats.** English spoken. Ask for Stephanie. Possibility to ship overseas

Cashmere & Pashmina

5012	Large selection of cashmere and pashmina
5016	Cashmere sweaters and shirts
5018	

Clothes

5016	Quality T-shirts
5017	Quality shirts
5072	Chinese dresses
5073	

17		Wide choice of good quality shirts
24	Bazaar	Wide choice of good quality shirts, jeans, jackets & coats
73		Various Chinese dresses and gifts

Fabric

06, 08, 09		Chinese silks
01		Table clothes, cushions
55, 81		Wide choice of Thai silks, 35-55 RMB/m
85A, 89A	FABRIC MARKET	Batiks, Jeans & fabric
100A		Bed sheets
98		Ballerina socks, 3p 100元
5123		Wide choice of fabric
5073		Chinese fabric, bags & dresses. +86 755 8232 3670
5141		Good quality fabric 136 9167 2130

Tea

5008	Said to be the best in Luohu, 136 0309 3573. See also Tea World page 38.
B-25	Bazaar stall 25. Good choice of tea pots, utensils, nuts, etc.

Restaurants

Arcadia Cantonese Restaurant

Laurel Restaurant

Arts

This artist does micro calligraphy on stones, the precision is unbelievable. You can get your name written in calligraphy. Very friendly Chinese calligrapher.

Luohu Shopping Index

Arts

JADE & CERAMICS
1F 1045, 1048
2F 2160, 2145, 2189
4F 4067, 4168
5F Next to the lift area

STATUES METAL & TERRACOTTA
1F 1010
3F 3139A , 3001A
4F 4060A

CHINESE PAPER-CUT
4F 4101A

BROIDERY
4F 4097

CALLIGRAPHY & NAME STAMPS
4F 4099, 4093A

PORTRAIT
4F 4056

CRYSTAL & STONE
2F Golden Square on the 2nd floor
4F 4066A

CHINESE BOXES AND GIFTS
3F 3196

MIRRORS & FRAMES
1F 1010
5F Bazaar 73

Bags

COSMETICS HANDBAGS
4F 4282

STYLISH-FASHIONABLE HANDBAGS
3F 3220, 3287A, 3155, 3176A, 3312A, 3223
4F 4069 , 4082, 4160A , 4073A

LUGGAGE & TRAVEL BAGS
2F 2271, 2010
3F 3292, 3192
4F 4170, 4296, 4073A

BACKPACKS
4F 4170, 4296

COMPUTER BAGS
2F 2010

EVENING BAGS
2F 2155
4F 4106

CHINESE TRADITIONAL HANDBAGS
2F 2021

CASUAL HANDBAGS & BAGS
4F 4160 , 4156A

RECOMMENDED QUALITY HANDBAGS
1F 1006, 1007, 1052, 1053
2F 240, 209, 2276, 2272, 2133, 2188
3F 3112, 3292, 3243, 3068
4F 4326

Beauty

MANICURE TOOL SETS
2F 2129

MANICURE
3F 3009-A1, 3313A
4F 4207

MASSAGE
1F 1001-1002, Massage Center, near exit 11
2F Massage Center, near CDH Cantonese Restaurant
3F Reflexology Center (3028), near BBC Restaurant
4F Massage, Manicure, and Pedicure Center (4028), near King Elephant Restaurant

HAIR SALON
4F Hair Salon (4293), near Liyuan Cantonese Restaurant

Belts
4F 4079, 4070, 4078, 4086

Cashmere & Pashmina
2F 272, 224, 2051, 2052
3F 3275
4F 4076, 4166, 4207
5F 5012, 5016, 5018

Clothes

BLUE JEANS & T-SHIRTS
1F 1050, 1089
2F 2050, 2139, 2221
3F 3147
4F 4083, 4333, 4107, 4160, 4290
5F 5016, 5017, 5072, BA17, BA24, BA73 (BA: Bazaar)

CHILDREN'S WEAR

1F	1089
2F	237, 2047
3F	3396A, 3297
4F	4110, 4197, 4168, 4068B, 4311A

WOMEN'S FASHION

3F	3182, 3118, 3069, 3067, 3309, 3190
4F	4145, 4308, 4416, 4121, 4197, 4085, 4338A

CHINESE TRADITIONAL

2F	298, 2021
3F	3146, 3098, 3009-A5, 3099A, 3125
4F	4438, 4117, 4068, 4288
5F	5073

UNDERWEAR

2F	2222
3F	3041
4F	4065, 4297, 4193, 4198, 4136, 4162

MEN'S TIES

2F	2139

OUTERWEAR

3F	3049A
4F	4206

GOLF

3F	3225
4F	4388

SOCKS

3F	3301
4F	4062, 4198

MEN'S FASHION

4F	4160, 4045, 4206

LEATHER

4F	4418, 4293, 4329

CAPS & HATS

4F	4101

TOWELS

4F	4388

Eye Glasses

3F	3268

Fabric

1F	1039-1042
5F	FM06, FM08, FM09, FM01, FM55, FM81, FM85A, FM89A, FM100A, FM98 (FM: Fabric Market)
	5123, 5073, 5141

Household Furnishings

1F	1039-1042
3F	3066

4F	4045, 4408J, 4422

Jewelry

2F	2128, 2259, 2G-39, 2G-47, 2G-22, 2G-11, 2G-24
	4090, 4167, 4160, 4296, 4066
3F	3029, 3282, 3154, 3154

Shoes

MEN & WOMEN - ALL STYLES

1F	1005
2F	273, 2133, 2045, 2152, 2159
3F	3095, 3062, 3255, 3257, 3131
4F	4337, 4335, 4197, 4388, 4062

DANCING SHOES

3F	3099A
4F	4135

CASUAL SHOES / SMART SHOES

3F	3099A
4F	4071A 4086

SPORT SHOES

3F	3239

CHINESE STYLE SHOES

2F	2048

Tailors

5F	5100, 5098, 5026, 5048, 5075, 5072, 5057, 5060A

Tea

5F	5008, B-25

Restaurants

1F	- Chinese Restaurant 大快活 (1090)
	- Chinese Restaurant 顺发阁 (1028)
2F	Cantonese CDH Restaurant
3F	Western BBC Restaurant (3008)
4F	- Liyuan Cantonese Restaurant (4238)
	- King Elephant Restaurant, Cantonese & Thai (4008)
5F	Laurel Restaurant

SHOPPING IN SHENZHEN

www.szCityGuide.com

深圳购物

The Shenzhen Silk Road Fantasy for Women

I JUST BOUGHT A pedometer that you clip around the ever-expanding middle-aged waistband. One evening of watching television, going to the kitchen for more nibbles and yet another glass of wine results in a magic total, and I repeat total of 14 steps. I think a dormouse probably spends more energy sleeping.

Now if you want to change your life-style, ladies, head for the Luohu border on the end of what used to be called the KRC (Kowloon Canton railway) line. Walk all day and evening (if you still have the energy) around the 5-storey megalopolis that is Luohu Commercial City.

As the train pulls up at Luohu, every woman I know is almost palpitating with excitement at the thought of all the silk brocades, the slippers, the pyjamas, the pearls, the watches and the handbags. For a sublimely decadent experience, head straight up in the lift to the 5th Floor if you crave fabric. Take all the time in the world as you finger and fondle the velvets and silks imagining yourself as some sort of Isadora Duncan in bewitching evening dress. The reality is somewhat more prosaic as they close at 8pm when you are only just beginning your silk road fantasy. Four words of warning:

- Do not buy the cheaper fabrics:

they will be synthetic and, ultimately, horrid to wear in a tropical climate.

- Be sure to buy at least half a metre more fabric than the tailor recommends as the estimates of one's avoirdupois can be misconceived when a Chinese lady judges how much fabric a European lady actually needs around the waistband.

- Take your favorite dress or skirt and have it copied in different fabrics: one, at least, will turn out successfully.

- Get a recommendation of a dressmaker in Shenzhen before you go because you will become extremely flustered as 20 people offer to do tailoring for you while you buy your delicious fabric.

- As to the watches, handbags, Tiffany key rings, luggage and shoes - they are all lovely but the watches break in one week; the handles fall off the handbags and luggage; and the shoes hurt as they are so badly made. But the pearls are the real thing and utterly beautiful.

So, ladies have a wonderful time and spend your money on having curtains, table cloths, napkins,

cushions and fabulous copies of your favorite dresses made up for you by curtain and upholstery shops and dressmakers. A restorative manicure, pedicure and/or massage will allow you to do lots more shopping. Try not to get upset by people pestering you (it helps to have headphones in your ears); head straight to the pearls on the 3rd floor; and then on to the exquisite paper butterflies and fabrics on the 5th floor.

Allow at least two hours for the pearls and three hours for the fabric and fittings. Take your pedometer with you so that you can measure how much exercise you are taking while shopping for essentials. Fall back onto the train feeling beautiful and virtuous. What a place, what an outing, what a treat...

■ Brought to you by
Heather Letterman
UIC

深圳购物指南

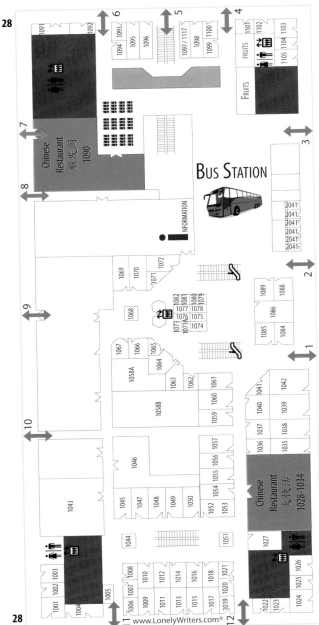

Chinese Restaurant 顺发阁 1090

BUS STATION

INFORMATION

Chinese Restaurant 大快活 1028-1034

FRUITS

FRUITS

Write down your own findings

1 F Circle out your favorite place on the floor map and jot down your findings.
Don't forget to register at www.szCityGuide.com to report your findings!

SHOPPING IN SHENZHEN

www.szCityGuide.com

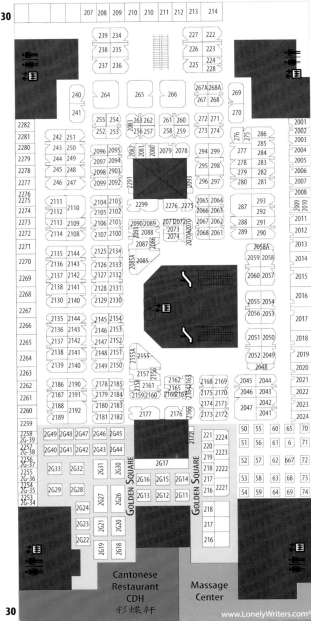

Cantonese
Restaurant
CDH
彩蝶轩

Massage
Center

深圳购物

2F

Circle out your favorite place on the floor map and jot down your findings.
Don't forget to register at www.szCityGuide.com to report your findings!

Shopping in Shenzhen

www.szCityGuide.com

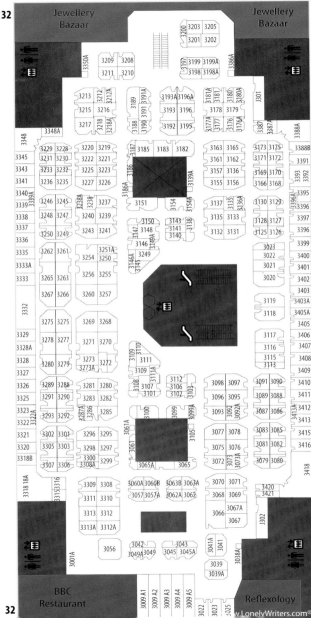

3F Circle out your favorite place on the floor map
and jot down your findings.
Don't forget to register at www.szCityGuide.com
to report your findings!

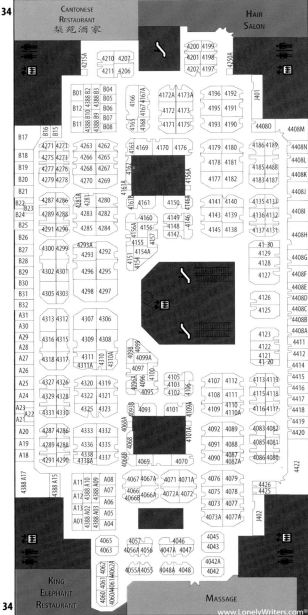

4F

Circle out your favorite place on the floor map
and jot down your findings.
Don't forget to register at www.szCityGuide.com
to report your findings!

SHOPPING IN SHENZHEN

www.szCityGuide.com

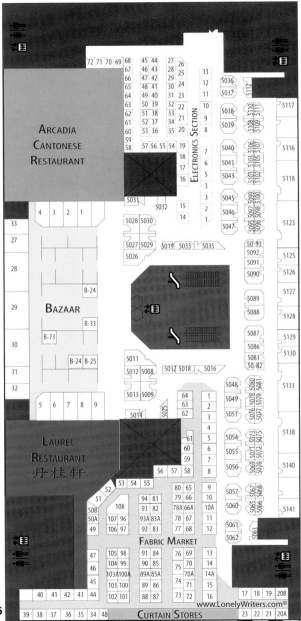

ARCADIA
CANTONESE
RESTAURANT

ELECTRONICS SECTION

BAZAAR

LAUREL
RESTAURANT
丹桂轩

FABRIC MARKET

CURTAIN STORES

www.LonelyWriters.com®

5F

Circle out your favorite place on the floor map and jot down your findings.
Don't forget to register at www.szCityGuide.com to report your findings!

Tea World in Luohu

I THOUGHT I WOULD be steeped in the tea experience. But nothing special really happened until... until I got to Shenzhen and went to Tea World. At Tea World, I bumped into some Chaozhou 潮州 people, and they brewed up Fenghuang Dancong 凤凰单枞 for me. They didn't do it in the traditional Chaozhou style of gongfu tea. But they used a gaiwan 盖碗 method, so I could taste the true nature of the tea; and appreciate the Qi of the tea. Well, they boiled 1 kettle full of water and brewed the tea from that single gaiwan of Dancong tea. Then, they boiled a second kettle of water for that same gaiwan of Dancong. I continued drinking. They boiled a third kettle of water for the same gaiwan of Dancong. I drank steep after steep after steep of the same infusion of leaf. I

wasn't counting, but it must have been over 20 infusions. They were about to boil a fourth kettle of water and continue brewing the same gaiwan, but I stopped at the end of the third kettle – because A: I had to go to the washroom; and B: I got smashingly tea drunk (although I had just eaten a heavy meal at McDonald's which is right next door to Tea World). I have to say, I have never gotten tea drunk like this before in my life. It was almost a narcotic-like experience (maybe – I don't actually know what narcotics are like.) But it sure felt strange – although I was still fully mentally aware. But then after that, it was much easier for other vendors to sell me their teas. I bought a bag of that Dancong 单枞 for my friends to try. Maybe they will get as tea drunk as I did. And I also bought 2 Sheng pu'er 生普洱 cakes from Ban Zhang factory. I have to admit, my puer collection is pretty shameful, so I need to grow my own personal inventory. If you want a really good tea experience, cross the border into Shenzhen, and experience Tea World.

■ Brought to you by Warren

Gaiwan Tea Preparation

The Chinese Gaiwan 盖碗 or covered cup is considered the preferred method for brewing teas with delicate flavors, such as green and white teas, but is suitable for any type of tea. This method has been used in China since about 1350. The gaiwan consists of a saucer, bowl and lid. The lid allows the tea to be infused right in the bowl and either be drunk right from the bowl or decanted into smaller tasting cups.

Tea World		茶叶世界
i	After exiting from Luohu Commercial City, head towards the Shangri-la hotel and cross the road. Once facing the hotel, keep going to your left for about 200 meters. Tea World is on the second floor of the Dexing building, next to McDonald's on Jianshe road.	
✉	2F, Dexing building, 47 Jianshe Rd	
	罗湖区建设路47号德兴大厦2楼	
☎	+86 755 8233 8664	

深圳购物

SHOPPING IN SHENZHEN

www.szCityGuide.com

Massage in Luohu

OFF TO SHENZHEN for a massage? This Mecca has become a top destination for massages. Assuming though that you are interested in a legitimate massage with trimmings, an excellent example of a night-trip from Hong Kong may include the following:

- Take the train to Luohu and cross the border. Once on the Shenzhen side, as you exit the main building with the Shangri-la in front of you, you should take a U-turn to bring you into the parking area of the Border Crossing building. Here you'll find a gathering of touts (with discount vouchers -- make sure to ask for them) for many of the more upper class spas/massage centres. You'll probably also see small clusters of customers waiting nearby for the free shuttle bus to take them for their evening of entertainment and relaxation. Choose your spa and join the crowd.

- The short but comfortable shuttle bus ride to the spa is often enlivened by the company of the other customers also looking forward to a night in their favorite massage centre. The mixture of patrons is quite eclectic, and a ride may have you sharing with a family of four, chattering excitedly about their impending family night out.

- On arrival at the spa, you'll normally receive the red-carpet treatment: legions of staff will simultaneously cheer "Huanying Guanglin 欢迎光临" (welcome) as your bags are carried, and you are ushered into the foyer of the spa. You'll then be given your locker key, and invited to proceed into the centre's changing rooms, and on to the main events!

- After changing out of your clothes and enjoying your shower, sauna, steam room, and jacuzzi, you will then be given a light pyjama-like set of clothes to wear while in the spa. Frequently, there will also be complementary partial laundry services (for underwear.)

- The next stage is to arrange your massage. In addition to what is usually an excellent massage with styles ranging from the ordinary (though very satisfying) "Chinese Style" to "Aromatherapy Style", there is often an array of extra facilities available to the visitor. In my own favorite centre, there are saunas, steam rooms, Jacuzzis, a gym, a cinema, an internet/computer area, an array of very nice reclining seats with

individual TVs, and many other amusements.

- The usually course is to pay for a 2-hour massage, after which you then have access to all the facilities for 24 hours (including a bed in the sleeping area). You can usually keep that room as a bedroom. There are of course VIP rooms with TV, mahjong, and other essentials.

- After the massage, it may be time for the complementary buffet dinner, following which a couple of hours spent lazily in a reclining armchair with personal TV may be just what is needed before retiring to bed. In the morning, after filling up again at the com-plementary breakfast buffet, you may decide it is time to return to the real world.

- Once showered and dressed (in the freshly laundered clothes), the shuttle bus will again whisk you back to the border where you can once again cross and resume life in Hong Kong.

The price? All of this is usually available at less than the price of a poor quality room in a 2 star hotel. At the time of writing, 120RMB was more than enough to cover the charges and tips!

■ Brought to you by
Dave Towey
UIC

Dongmen 1001 Shopping Streets

Credits 韦洪兴

MOST DAY-TRIPPERS TO Shenzhen make the mistake of not venturing beyond Luohu. There is a lot more to shopping in Shenzhen than just Luohu Commercial City. Only two stops on the Metro to Laojie Station - 老街站 will take you to the busy maze of pedestrian streets that is Dongmen. Take Exit "A" and head towards a group of traditional Chinese-style buildings. Here you'll find the first ever McDonald's in China (opened in 1990)! Nearby is the Sun Plaza, a big shopping centre full of name brands. In the surrounding lanes you'll find loads of Chinese brands.

Culture Square 文化广场 is a good place to sit and people watch when the pace becomes too hectic. For another kind of culture head to Boya Arts City 博雅艺术城. Here you'll find

musical instruments, art supplies, including calligraphy brushes, picture framing and a bookstore specializing in art books (some in English.)

Across the road is Hongji Handicraft City 鸿基工艺城. The first floor offers mainly small items of jade, teapots, brass, fountains and water features. On the second floor you'll find larger works of art such as sculpture and vases.

The Dongmen area is one of the oldest parts of Shenzhen. It was established about 300 years ago, leading it to be alternatively known as "Laojie", or "Old Street" 老街.

Dongmen is accessible from exits to the Laojie metro station 老街站 and lies just north of Shennan Dong Road. "Dongmen" usually refers to more than just "Dongmen Road", encompassing the entire series of con-

Fashion

AT DONGMEN, THERE are numerous small shops selling original brands such as Nike, Adidas, Rebook, and such. Prices for those are about the same as you would pay in Hong Kong. If you are looking for great bargain as you would in Luohu Commercial City, there are a few places you can go to: Kowloon City Shopping Center for its wide range of women's clothing, New Women's City for higher quality women's wear, Xihua Shopping Palace for electronic gadgets and teenager clothing, and Dongmen Shoe City for a wide range of shoes.

Kowloon City Shopping Centre	九龙城广场
New Women's City	新女人商城
Dongmen Shoe City	东门鞋城
Xihua Shopping Palace	西华宫购物中心
Baohua Lou	宝华楼
Nantang & Zhongwei	南唐、中威
Baima Fabric Market	白马布料市场

深圳购物指南

Credits 唐致意

KOWLOON CITY SHOPPING Centre is packed with Chinese products mainly targeted to women. The Chinese locals say that you get the same kind of experience as in Luohu Commercial Center but with cheaper prices. Here you need to bargain. Seven floors with no fixed prices, you can find it all: women's wear, hats, manicure, watches, movies, etc...

Kowloon City Shopping Centre						九龙城广场
F	1F	Cosmetics Home Appliances Digital Equipment Jewelry & Ornaments Local Taste	3F	Trendy Clothing Ornaments Shoes & Hats Watches Movies	5F	Bridal Suite Cosmetics Beauty Salon Hairdressing Manicure
	2F	Trendy Clothing Ornaments Shoes & Hats Watches Movies	4F	Cosmetics Beauty Salon Hairdressing Manicure	6F 7F	Body Massage Beauty Salon Hairdressing Manicure
✉	No. 2013 Dongmen Zhonglu, next the Dongmen bridge; refer to the Dongmen Area map, pages 44-45. 罗湖区东门中路2013号					
☏	+86 755 2516 2536					
🚌	Bus: 1, 3, 5, 103. MTR: Laojie Station - 老街站					
⏳	10am - 10pm					

Credits 唐軟佳

Credits 林珠

Nᴇᴡ ᴡᴏᴍᴇɴ's ᴡᴏʀʟᴅ is a modern and clean one-storey department store mainly targeted to women, selling mainly Chinese brands, good quality products at very reasonable prices.

New Women's City	新女人商城
2F	Women's wear Women's underwear Kids wear Wedding dresses Men's wear
✉	Buxing Jie, Dongmen, Luohu District, next to Dongmen Shoe City; refer to the Dongmen Area map, pages 44-45. 罗湖区东门步行街
☎	+86 755 8222 2896
🚌	Bus: 1, 3, 5, 103 MTR: Laojie Station - 老街站
⧖	weekdays: 10am-10:30pm weekends: 10am-11:00pm

Shoes

Credits 唐秋愁

Credits 林珠

DONGMEN SHOE CITY is a modern and clean 2-storey department store selling shoes and sportswear. Mainly Chinese brands, good quality products at very reasonable prices.

Dongmen Shoe City					东门鞋城
F	2F	City Shoes Casual Shoes Sport Shoes	3F	Sport Shoes Sportswear	
✉	Buxing Jie, Dongmen, Luohu District, next to Women's World; refer to the Dongmen Area map, pages 44-45. 罗湖区东门步行街				
☏	+86 755 8222 2988				
🚌	Bus: 1, 3, 5, 103 MTR: Laojie Station - 老街站				
⏳	10am-10pm				

CHECK THE Chinese Corner section at the end of this chapter to learn some Chinese vocabulary when buying computers & electronics.

Credits 唐毅楼

FIRST FLOOR ARE electronic goods, mp3 , watches, electronic dictionaries, game boys, psp, etc. 2nd floor and above sell clothes, mostly for teenagers.

Here you can buy shoes, dresses, underwear, socks, etc. Prices range between 15 and 100RMB. Watches 15-200RMB.

Xihua Shopping Palace				西华宫购物中心
F	1F	Electronic goods	2F-5F	Clothes
✉	Buxing Jie, Dongmen, Luohu District, next to next to McDonalds; refer to the Dongmen Area map, pages 44-45. 罗湖区东门步行街			
🚌	Bus: 1, 3, 5, 103 MTR: Laojie Station - 老街站			
⏳	09:00 - 22:00			

SIMILAR TO XIHUA Palace 西华宫, Baohua Lou comprise several stationery shops,

clothes, hair dressing, scarf, belts, stationery, stocks, underwear, CDs, etc.

Baohua Lou		宝华楼
✉	Located next to Xihua Palace 西华宫. When facing Xihua Palace 西华宫, it's on your right hand side; refer to the Dongmen Area map, pages 44-45. 罗湖区东门步行街	
🚌	Bus: 1, 3, 5, 103. MTR: Laojie Station - 老街站	
⏳	10:30am-10:30pm	

Credits 林琛

Credits 林琛

MOST CHINESE PEOPLE prefer clothes in these two places, Nantang and Zhongwei. Clothes are better quality and nicer look. Prices range between 30 and 400RMB, but for 100RMB you can get something descent. These two places sell also shoes, belts and underwear. Like at Xihua Palace, Nantang & Zhongwei are more targeted to young crowd 15~25.

Nantang & Zhongwei				南唐、中威
F	1F	Electronic goods	2F-5F	Clothes
✉	Located in the heart of Dongmen Streets, next to McDonalds; refer to the Dongmen Area map, pages 44-45. 罗湖区东门步行街			
🚌	Bus: **1, 3, 5, 103.** MTR: **Laojie Station -** 老街站			
⌛	11am - 10pm			

Don't forget to register at WWW.SZCITYGUIDE.COM
to report your findings!

BAIMA FABRIC MARKET 白马布料市场 is targeted mostly to an older crowd. This 6-floor mall is facing the Culture Square. Don't expect any information written in English. You should bargain but prices are low.

Baima Fabric Market					白马布料市场
F	B1	Clothing, jewelry, children wear, Jeans, handbags, leather goods, women's underwear	2F	Women fashion ♥ 2206 for Women underwear and 2217 for ethnic clothes	4F	Men's wear
	1F	Clothing, shoe square	3F	Men's fashion and underwear	5F	Export Lifestyle ♥ 5003 T-shirts
✉	Next to the Culture Square and KFC. 罗湖区东门文化广场即到		⧖	11am - 9pm		

IF IN DONGMEN and looking for Jewels, shoppers normally go to Shuibei 东门水贝珠宝 (see page 119). There might be a better deal for you, however. Try this tiny shop selling gold, k-gold and silver. With more than 20 years' experience, Jinyizhu Shoushi 金艺珠首饰 is mostly specialized in making rings. Here prices tend to be lower than other places.

Jewels at Dongmen	珠宝
✉	No. 19, Tianfu Building, Lixin Garden, Shaibu Road, Luohu. Behind the McDonald's next to MOI Shopping Center. 罗湖区晒布路立新花园天富楼19号
⧖	9am - 9pm
☏	+86 755 8220 6698. For English speaker call Annie at 135 7085 0971

Fabric

Aᴌᴌ ғᴀʙʀɪᴄ ᴍᴀʀᴋᴇᴛs operate in the same way. There are many small stores under the same roof, each operating separately. Be sure to bargain. Some shop assistants may speak some English, but most do not. The fabric is measured in meters. The selection is amazing, the prices will make you smile. Curtains and upholstery shops will make your curtains/blinds and shades if you want. Pictures or drawings are helpful, but there are lots of design samples in the shop. Bring your measurements. Most shops have many fabric sample books for ordering.

Consider having your bedding custom made. Mattresses need to be measured tall/wide/deep. Huge selection of styles and fabrics

Baima Olympic Market   奥运城新白马布料

Dongmen Fabric and Curtain Market   东门布料窗帘广场

Other Fabric places in Dongmen   其它布料广场

ALSO KNOWN AS Olympic Fabric Market 奥运城新白马布料, Baima Fabric Market is one of the great places to shop for fabric and accessories. 1st and 2nd floors of this building are fabric markets. Many are wholesale shops and do not sell by the meter (if there are small clips of fabric on all wall, it's wholesale), but there are some retail shops here as well. Floors 3-6 sell ribbon, trim, buttons, beads and many other accessories. Prices for ribbon and trim are even better than on the fabric markets.

Baima Olympic Market	奥运城新白马布料

	♥ Expats' recommendations	

F	THREAD & ZIP
	   3F 3055
	   4F 4008
	BELTS
	   3F 3041
	BUTTONS
	   3F 3053B
	   4F 4032
	BELT CLIPS
	   3F 3054
	   4F 4003
	RIBBONS & ROPES
	   4F 4033
		FRAMES & MOTIFS WITH PEARLS
		   4F 4061, 4002A
		TIES
		   2F 2008
		CURTAINS
		   2F 2039
		BROIDERY
		   4F 4066-4067 (choose your material and go to the 1st floor to have it tailored)
		CRYSTAL DECORATION
		   4F 4050

✉	From MOI Shopping center, go opposite direction of the Dongmen foot-bridge, after you pass by the old Haiya department store. Baima Fabric Market is on your left, next to the overpass. 罗湖区东门中奥运城新白马布料市场	
🚌	Bus: 1, 3, 5, 103. MTR: Laojie Station - 老街站	
⏳	10am - 10pm	

SHOPPING IN SHENZHEN

www.szcityguide.com

深圳购物

Credits /唐春德

Credits /林荣

DONGMEN FABRIC MARKET which once was the best place to shop for fabric is getting older, most of the shops are migrating slowly to newer buildings in the heart of the Dongmen area. In August 2008, the New Baima department store located opposite the culture square will be the next destination to shop for Fabric. In the meantime, Dongmen Fabric Market still offers a good alternative. There are many small stores operating under the same roof. Some shops may speak some English but most shops do not. Fabric is measured by the meter. Curtains and upholstery shops make your curtains/blinds/shades if you want. Pictures or drawings are helpful, but there are lots of design samples in the shops. Bring your measurements. Most shops have many fabric sample books for ordering. This market is a lot larger and less crowded than Luohu Commercial City Fabric Market. You should bargain but prices are reasonable, around 20RMB/meter.

Dongmen Fabric and Curtain Market		东门布料窗帘广场		
F	2F	Beddings, Bead Door Curtain, Korean Dress and Personal Adornment, Vinyl Wallpaper, Supplementary Material & Household Appliances ♥ Shop 5: Sequin, pearls, stones, all kind of buttons and decorative items for clothing	4F	Curtain Fabric Tablecloths Coverings Sofa sets Hotel clothes	Herbal Products Beauty Salon Hair Salon Foot Massage Gourmet Tea
				♥ Shops 50/13: Blinds: wooden, silk colorful; 05 good choice of tea and teaware	
	3F	Curtain, Beddings, Fashion material, Art performance apparel ♥ Shops: 323: Silk; 07 Ribbon; 123; 103 Chinese silk, 61 Beddings; B1 party costumes, Ethnic Chinese clothing; 29 Curtain, Chinese Fabric, Beddings	5F	Curtains, Tablecloths	Hotel clothes Sofa sets
				♥ Shops: 53/ 45/ 33: Good quality blinds	

深圳购物

Dongmen Fabric and Curtain Market　　东门布料窗帘广场

✉	Coming from Dongmen Rd., cross the Dongmen footbridge and head towards the wet market, Dongmen fabric market is above it. Refer to the Dongmen Area map, pages 44-45. 东门布料窗帘广场，湖贝路
🚌	Bus: 1, 3, 5, 103 MTR: Laojie Station - 老街站
⏳	10am - 6pm

Credits 唐报愁感

Credits 林焘

AROUND THE DONGMEN Fabric Market are several malls selling curtains, fabric, blinds, etc.

The 2-storey building "Curtains World 窗帘世界" opposite is a good place to shop for curtains & fabric.

Other Fabric places in Dongmen　　其它布料广场

✉	Hubei Rd., opposite Dongmen Fabric Market. Refer to the Dongmen Area map, pages 44-45. 罗湖区湖贝路兴华广场
🚌	Bus: 1, 3, 5, 103 MTR: Laojie Station - 老街站
⏳	10am - 6pm

CHECK THE Chinese Corner section at the end of this chapter to learn some Chinese vocabulary when buying computers & electronics.

SHOPPING IN SHENZHEN

WWW.SZCITYGUIDE.COM

深圳购物

SHOPPING IN SHENZHEN

www.szCityGuide.com

Arts

Credits 唐毅德

Credits 唐毅德

A T BOYA ARTS City you will find musical instruments, art supplies, including calligraphy brushes, picture framing and a bookstore specializing in art books (some in English.)

Boya Arts City				深圳博雅艺术
F	1F	Paintings, Teaware, Frames, etc.	4F	Arts, Chinese paintings Jade work
	2F	Carving, Chinese vases, sculptures, etc.	5F	Piano seller, music lessons
	3F	Musical Instruments Book store		
✉	Floors 3-5, No. 6 Lixin Rd. After passing MOI Shopping Center, turn left. Boya Arts City is on your right hand side; refer to the Dongmen Area map, pages 44-45. 罗湖区立新路6号3-5楼			
⌛	Floors 1, 2, 4, & 5: 10am - 6h30pm Floor 3: 10am - 9pm			
☎	+86 755 8222 9508			
🖱	www.pokart.com sales@pokart.com			

Credits 唐浩德

Credits 林深

OPPOSITE BOYA ARTS City is Hongji Handicraft City. The second floor offers mainly small items of jade, teapots, brass fountains and water features. On the third floor you'll find larger pieces of art such as sculpture and vases.

Hongji Handicraft City				鸿基工艺城
F	2F	Small items of jade, teapots, brass fountains and water features	4F	Eye glasses, sun glasses
	3F	Art work, sculptures, vases.		
✉	Hongji Gongyicheng. After passing MOI Shopping Center, turn left. Hongji Handicraft City is on your left hand side, opposite Boya Arts City; refer to the Dongmen Area map, pages 44-45. 罗湖区立新路6号 东门鸿基工艺城 2-4楼			
🚌	Bus: 1, 3, 5, 103 MTR: Laojie Station - 老街站			
⧗	10am - 9pm			

Shopping Malls

Credits 唐毅德

Credits 唐毅德

SUN PLAZA IS a large six-storey shopping center carrying well known brands such as Converse, Crocs, Esprit. Prices are fixed but reasonable. Park's Shop and Starbucks are also here.

Sun Plaza					太阳广场
F	B1	Large Park'n Shop ♥ Beauty products like Nivea, Neutrogena. Kitchen houseware, luggage, wine, soft drink, fresh fish, large choice of nuts, Mc Cormick spices, Almond Cake from Macau, Balsamic Vinegar.	3F	Women clothing, underwear, maternity, leather collection, Croissants de France ♥ Underwear Triumph, Wacoal; Yves Saint Laurent luggage, Croissants de France has a large seat area and has not only many pastries but a wide choice of salted dishes	
	1F	Large shoe space ♥ Some high quality walking shoes, Courber Walking shoes, Bata store has a large space.	4F	Men's wear, casual wear, casual bags ♥ Wranger/ Pierre Cardin/ Levis/ Lee Men's wear, Lacoste, Adidas, Nike shoes and clothes	
	2F	Women's clothing, cosmetics ♥ Esprit watches and clothes	5F	Sportswear, children wear, beddings, furniture ♥ Converse/Puma/ Crocs/ New Balance shoes and clothing	
			6F	Cinema, playroom, bookstore, bar	
✉	2001 Jiefang Road, Dongmen, Luohu; refer to the Dongmen Area map, pages 44-45. 罗湖区东门解放路2001号				
⧖	Mon-Thu 10am - 10pm, Fri-Sun 10am - 11:30pm				

Credits 唐贵德

Credits 林深

RAINBOW DEPARTMENT STORE is another large multi storey shopping mall, similar to MOI Shopping plaza 茂业百货.

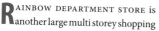

Rainbow Department Store				天虹商场	
F	1F	Supermarket Pharmacy Tea, Tobacco & Wine Miscellaneous articles	4F	Women's Dress Underwear Home Furnishings Sewing Services	
	2F	Cosmetics, Jewelry Watch & Clock, Shoes Glasses, Bag & Luggage Shoes Repair Watch & Clock Repair center	5F	Men's Clothing Leisure Clothing Sportswear Fitness Equipment	
	3F	Girl's Dress Leisure Clothing Ornament Beauty Centre	6F	Electrical Appliances Digital Products, Stationery AV Products, Office Equipment Hardware, Children's Clothes Beddings, Children Playground	
✉	17 Xinyuanlu, Dongmen Luohu; refer to the Dongmen Area map, pages 44-45. 罗湖区新园路17号				
⧗	Weekdays: 9am - 10pm Weekends: 9am - 10h30pm				
✆	+86 755 8235 1315, 823 5140				
🖱	www.china-llsun.com				

MOI SHOPPING CENTER 茂业百货 has several similar department stores in Shenzhen and Zhuhai. MOI Department Store sells a wide range of affordable jewelry, garments and cosmetics. A number of world famous brands are available, such as Chanel, SK-II and some other high quality cosmetics.

MOI Shopping Center					茂业百货
F	B1	Supermarket	6F	Hobby & Leisure Town	
	1F	Hips & Trendy Town	7F	Sport House	
	2F	Miss Shop	8F	Mum & Kids	
	3F	Young Fashion	9F	Household Square	
	4F	Elegant Fashion	10F	Home Appliances	
	5F	World Label Men's Wear	11F	Delicacy Square	
✉	2047 Dongmen Road Center. Next to the Dongmen foot-bridge, refer to the Dongmen map, pages 44-45. 罗湖区东门中路2047号				
🚌	Bus: 1, 3, 5, 103 MTR: Laojie Station - 老街站				
⌛	09am - midnight				
☎	+86 755 2516 2613				
🖱	www.maoye.cn/moien				

Kitchen equipment

Credits 林染

CAQ IS A 4-floor kitchen equip-ment store located opposite Dongmen Fabric Market, selling mostly to hotels and restaurants, but also to private households. Fixed prices, good quality.

CAQ Kitchen Equipment				厨安居
F	1F	Large choice of cooking ceramic pots.	3F	Hotel and Restaurant equipment, Kitchen Aid Classic.
	2F	Kitchen equipment : Coffee machines, Blenders, Juice Blenders. Indoor/outdoor thermometers, plain plates & Chinese colored style, Chine Bone White porcelain.	4F	Pastry pans and plastic containers.
✉	2163 Hubei Rd., Dongmen, Luohu; refer to the Dongmen Area map, pages 44-45. 罗湖区湖贝路2163号东门广场			
⌛	10am - 7pm			
☎	+86 755 8883 8182			
🖱	www.caq.cc (Chinese) / caqsky@163.com			

Staying overnight in Dongmen

Credits 林杰

THE METROPOLE HOTEL in Dongmen Rd. is often recommended by foreigners coming to Shenzhen shopping over a weekend. It is only 3 minute walk to Dongmen pedestrian shopping area. The rooms are serviced apartments with kitchenette and lounge. Buffet breakfast costs 50RMB. A one-hour massage in your hotel room costs 70RMB. Very friendly and accommodating staff. Its location is excellent - cross the footbridge over Dongmen Rd., pass McDonald's and the massive pedestrian shopping area; it's a right turn, only metres away. The Metropole hotel has free transport to and from Luohu station.

Metropole Hotel   维景京华酒店公寓

- Distance to Shenzhen International international airport: 40 Km
- Distance to Luohu Railway Station: 3 Km
- Baby sitting service, Business centre, Cocktail bar, Currency exchange, Gymnasium, Internet access, Laundry facilities, Parking facilities, Restaurant, Room service, Sauna
- US$50-70 per night

Metropole Hotel   维景京华酒店公寓

✉	Metropole Service Apartment Hotel Shenzhen, 2088, Dongmen Road C, Luohu 罗湖区东门中路2088号
🚌	Bus: 1, 3, 5, 103 MTR: Laojie Station - 老街站
☎	+86 755 8231 8388
🖱	www.metropolesz.com

Credits 唐晓伟

Huaqiang Bei Area, Electronics & Women's World

Credits 韦洪兴

Sᴉɴᴄᴇ ᴛʜᴇ ᴏᴘᴇɴɪɴɢ of Huaqiang World 华强世界, the Huaqiang Bei area 华强北, together with the giant SEG/Saige 赛格 and Huaqiang Electronics Plaza 华强电子广场, is the biggest electronics shopping area in China.

Getting to Huaqiang Bei 华强北 isn't difficult. Take the MTR and get off at Huaqiang Lu Station Exit A 华强路站A出口, turn left, follow the crowd, go up the escalator and keep going straight. You will soon hit Huaqiang road 华强路. Look up and you'll see SEG, the most famous electronic market.

The question is: where to buy what? Through the interviews we conducted, we realized that Chinese customers have great habits when shopping at Huaqiang Bei. In short, for branded computers go to SEG floors 4-7 or Huaqiang Electronics World across the road floors 3-6. For second-hand computers go to Huaqiang Electronics Plaza 华强电子广场 floors 3-5, computer parts like LCD, chips, CPU, RAM, etc. are there. You can even get your faulty chip on your video card replaced! There are also really cheap and old 2nd hand computers at the Foreign Market.

Looking for mobile phones? For a safe choice with warranty, go to Gome 国美, Sundan 顺电, or Suning 苏宁. Xieheng 协亨, Holpe 恒波, and iTell 易天 offer better deals as there are specialized mobile phone retailers. Best deals in China are undoubtedly at Yuangwang Digital City 远望数码城, a 4-floor building packed with mobile phone wholesale retailers who offer best prices in China but without warranty.

For high performance speakers, home theater systems, table radios, multimedia systems and such, go to Wanshang Electronics City 万商电器成, 2nd floor.

Ladies will also find great places to shop for fashion, jewels, cosmetics or kids wear. One of the ladies' favorite places is the Foreign Trade Clothing Market which carries big size clothes and shoes. Behind this market there is a tiny foreign book store that sells books for kids. At MOI Shopping Center 茂业百货 you will find all the major cosmetic brands such as MAC, Chanel, Dior...

Huaqiang Bei quick shopping advice table

For quick reference while shopping, we compiled the table next page. Refer to the corresponding section to get further details.

Note: This table is the result of interviews with professionals as well as shoppers. To make sure of the accuracy of the information, we interviewed both Chinese and Westerners. We decided not to mention places that where too far off Huanqiang bei Road as there are plenty of choices in that area to get the best deals.

■ Brought to you by
Adriano Lucchese 唐毅德
www.LonelyWriters.com 瓏玲作家

Getting to Huaqiang Bei

🚌 MTR: Get off at Huaqiang Lu station - 华强路站 and leave from exit A, walk strait and turn left, you will be along Huaqiang Rd.
Bus: many buses pass by Huanqiang bei: K113, 9, 12, 209, 212

Huaqiang Bei quick shopping advice table

	① Saige/SEG Computer Market	⑩ Saige/SEG Digital Market	⑱ Huaqiang Electronic World	㉑ Huaqiang Electronic Plaza	④ Saibo Digital Plaza
Computers (Bran new)	✔	✔	✔		✔
Computer parts, Hardware, DIY...	✔			✔	
Computer peripherals, Printers, scanners...	✔	✔	✔	✔	✔
Digital equipment, MP3/MP4, USB, CF/SD...		✔			✔
Digital cameras	✔	✔	✔		✔
Electronic components	✔		✔	✔	
2nd hand computers	✔			✔	
Mobile phones					✔
Hi-fi systems, Home theater					
Security & Protection devices					

深圳购物

SHOPPING IN SHENZHEN

www.szCityGuide.com

深圳购物

SHOPPING IN SHENZHEN

www.szCityGuide.com

(8)(9)(12) Gome Sundan Suning	(6) Yuanwang Digital City	(20) iTell Xieheng Holpe	(7) Wanshang Electronics City	(3) International Electronics Market	(2) Protection & Security Market
✓					
			✓		
✓			✓		
✓				✓	
✓				✓	
✓	✓	✓			
✓			✓		
				✓	✓

深圳购物

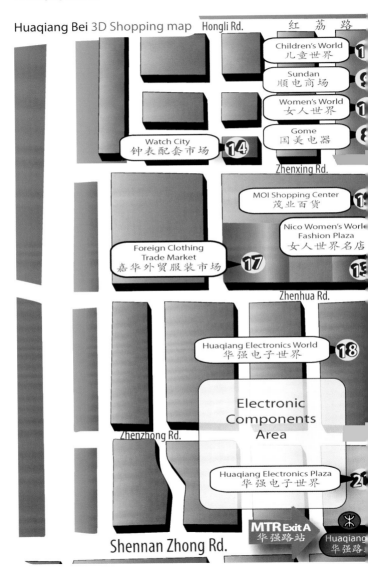

Huaqiang Bei 3D Shopping map Hongli Rd. 红 荔 路

Children's World
儿童世界

Sundan
顺电商场

Women's World
女人世界

Gome
国美电器

Watch City
钟表配套市场 **14**

Zhenxing Rd.

MOI Shopping Center
茂业百货

Nico Women's World
Fashion Plaza
女人世界名店

Foreign Clothing
Trade Market
嘉华外贸服装市场 **17**

Zhenhua Rd.

Huaqiang Electronics World
华强电子世界 **18**

Electronic
Components
Area

Zhenzhong Rd.

Huaqiang Electronics Plaza
华强电子世界 **2**

MTR Exit A
华强路站

Huaqiang
华强路

Shennan Zhong Rd.

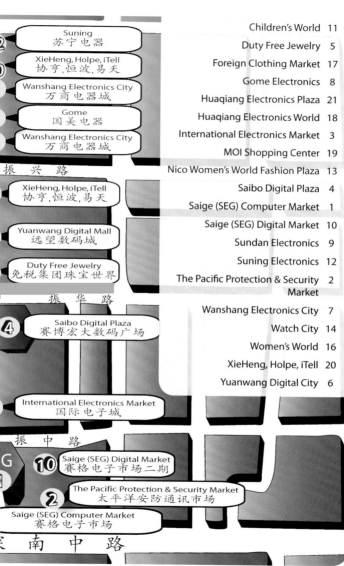

Children's World 11
Duty Free Jewelry 5
Foreign Clothing Market 17
Gome Electronics 8
Huaqiang Electronics Plaza 21
Huaqiang Electronics World 18
International Electronics Market 3
MOI Shopping Center 19
Nico Women's World Fashion Plaza 13
Saibo Digital Plaza 4
Saige (SEG) Computer Market 1
Saige (SEG) Digital Market 10
Sundan Electronics 9
Suning Electronics 12
The Pacific Protection & Security 2
Market
Wanshang Electronics City 7
Watch City 14
Women's World 16
XieHeng, Holpe, iTell 20
Yuanwang Digital City 6

Huaqiang Bei Table of Contents

Computers & Electronic Components

Computers & Electronic Components   电脑、电子

2nd hand computers and accessories   二手电脑

Mobile Phones & Accessories   手机、手机配件

Audio-Video & Electronics   音响、电子

Other Products   其它产品

Women & Children

Children's World   儿童世界

Nico Women's World Fashion Plaza   女人世界名店

MOI Shopping Center   茂业百货

Women's World   女人世界

Foreign Trade Clothing Market   嘉华外贸服装市场

Duty Free Jewelry   免税集团珠宝世界

Computers & Electronic Components

电脑、电子

The Giant Saige (SEG)

赛格

SEG ELECTRONICS MARKET, established in Huaqiang Bei road in 1988, is housed in three buildings, the SEG Computer Market ①, the SEG Electronics Market, and the third one functions as the SEG Digital Market ⑩.

Behind Huaqiang Electronics Plaza ㉑ and Huaqiang Electronics World ⑱ are many old and newer buildings dealing with electronic components. Refer to the map pages 70-71, "Electronic Components Area."

Did you know?

Huaqiangbei is the biggest computers, mobile phones, and electronic components trading market in China.

Credits 唐敦德

Credits 唐敦德

WHO HASN'T HEARD of Saige (SEG) Computer Market is most probably not into computers. Up until recently, SEG was the top destination to shop for computers and accessories. Since

the new Huaqiang Electronic World, shoppers have now a wider choice. The ten-storey Saige (SEG) Computer Market has every imaginable part of a computer or communication device you can imagine.

❶ Saige (SEG) Computer Market

赛格电子市场

❶ Saige (SEG) Computer Market　　赛格电子市场

F					
	1F	Electronic components	6F	Computer accessories DIY, 2nd hand computers, 2nd hand printers + Repair center	
	2F		7F	DIY computers & accessories 2nd hand computers, cables	
	3F	Branded computers Printers, scanners, laptop, digital cameras, video projectors, GPS, SD/CF/USB, UPS Toshiba, Philips, Canon, Sony, etc.	8F	DYI computers & accessories 2nd hand computers, cables, CPU coolers (stall 8101)	
	4F	Branded computers Laptop, motherboards, printers, fax, display monitors, desktops	9F	DIY computers & accessories 2nd hand computers, cables Cat7	
	5F	Computer accessories DIY, 2nd hand computers, 2nd hand printers	10F	DIY computers & accessories	

i
- Many of the stalls have prices displayed but it is still acceptable to bargain. If there are no prices displayed it is highly advisable to bargain. Examine what you are purchasing very carefully and ask for a receipt.
- SEG Electronics Market also sells 2nd computers accessories. Check the opposite building Huaqiang Electronics Plaza ㉑ for wider choice of 2nd hand computers and computer accessories.
- It is also possible to have electronic products repaired on the 5th floor and above.

♥ Saige (SEG) is said to be people's favorite place to shop for desktop computers, laptop, printers and computer accessories. Check also its biggest newly established competitor across the street, Huaqiang Electronics World ⑱

save $ To have an rather good idea on how much money to spend on your next buy, check the computers and computer parts prices at www.segem.com.cn (Chinese), and minus off 10%.

✉ Saige Dianzi Shichang, Huaqiangbei, Futian. Refer to the map pages 70-71.
福田区华强北赛格电子市场

⌛ 9am – 6pm

🚌 MTR: Huaqiang Lu Station - 华强路站. Bus: 9, 12, 209, 212

🖱 www.segem.com.cn (Chinese)

Credits 唐毅德

SEG DIGITAL MARKET is a good place to shop for entertainment devices like MP3s, MP4s, USBs, personal stereos and DVD players. Besides computer hardware and software, SEG also sells just about every electronic-related product imaginable from telephone leads to RC toys.

⑩ **Saige (SEG) Digital Market**				赛格电子市场二期
F	1F	Branded laptop & desktops Nikon camera shop	2F	Printers, printers cartridge and recharges, USB CF/SD, etc.
			3F	MP3/MP4, Digital, cables, computer parts, etc.
i	Many of the stalls have prices displayed but it is still acceptable to bargain. If there are no prices displayed it is highly advisable to bargain. Examine what you are purchasing very carefully and ask for a receipt.			
✉	Saige Dianzi Shichang, phase II, Huaqiang bei. Refer to the map pages 70-71. 华强北赛格电子市场二期			
🚌	MTR: Huaqiang Lu Station - 华强路站 Bus: 9, 12, 209, 212			
⏱	9am - 6pm			

Did you know?

Saige (SEG) is the second highest building in shenzhen and the highest steel tube concrete building in the world with 355.8 meters tall.

深圳购物

SHOPPING IN SHENZHEN

www.szCityGuide.com

The Uprising Giant: Huaqiang World   华强世界

LいKE THE SAIGE (SEG) group, the Huaqiang Group offers electronic components and electronic equipment as well as computer products. Until very recently however, the Saige (SEG) Group, with its 3 buildings has been the leader in the electronics industry around the HuaqiangBei Area. With Huaqiang Electronics World 华强电子世界 ⑱, the Huaqiang World Group accounts a total of 3 buildings that largely compete with the Giant Saige (SEG).

THIS BUILDING IS the newly opened Huaqiang World. 6 floors packed with electronic components, computers and computer accessories. Like its competitor Saige (SEG), you will find great deals here. If your goal is to shop for computers and computers parts, head directly to the 4th floor.

⑱ **Huaqiang Electronics World**			华强电子世界	
F	1F	Electronic components	4F	Computers and computer parts, printers, LCD display, desktops, MP3, MP4, digital equipment, etc.
	2F		5F	
	3F		6F	
i	Many of the stalls have prices displayed on their products but it is still acceptable to bargain. Refer to the map pages 70-71.			
☏	9am - 6pm			
🚌	MTR: Huaqiang Lu Station - 华强路站. Bus: 9, 12, 209, 212			
☏	+86 755 8329 4262			
🖱	www.hqew.com/En/			

Credits 唐锐德

Credits 唐锐德

THIS BUILDING IS rather old. It is still, however, a very good place to shop for 2nd hand computers and computer accessories. For wider choices, check it's bigger brother, the newly opened Huaqiang Electronics World ⑱

㉑	**Huaqiang Electronics Plaza**				华强电子广场
F	1F	Electronic components	5F	Computers and computer parts, all possible computer parts you can name, they have it!	
	2F		6F		
	3F	Computers and computer parts, printers, LCD display, desktops, MP3, MP4, digital equipment, etc.			
	4F				
i	Good place to buy 2nd hand accessories, laptop and desktops. You can easily have any chips on a faulty motherboard replaced here. When there are no prices displayed, it is advisable to bargain.				
🚌	MTR: Huaqiang Lu Station - 华强路站 Bus: 9, 12, 209, 212				
⌛	9am - 6pm				

Other Computer Shopping Places 其它地方

Credits 语数场

SAIBO DIGITAL PLAZA is specialized in branded computer desktops, laptop and printers/scanners, etc. On the 3rd and 4th floors are mobile phones, memory cards, DVDs, and some computer accessories.

❹ **Saibo Digital Plaza**	赛博宏大数码广场
i	Apple store located on the 2nd floor next to the escalator
❤	On the 3th floor next to the escalator there is a good O₂ mobile phone retailer. Offers a good alternative to phone without warranty. - 1 month warranty < 4000 RMB - 12 months > 4000 RMB Contact: +86 133 1689 3938
✆	+86 755 8328 1442
🚌	MTR: Huaqiang Lu Station - 华强路站 Bus: 9, 12, 209, 212
⧗	Sunday to Thursday 9am-6:30pm Friday & Saturday 9am-9pm

CHECK THE Chinese Corner section at the end of this chapter to learn some Chinese vocabulary when buying computers & electronics.

Credits 唐教德

Credits 唐教德

GOME, SUNDAN OR Suning is a good alternative for customers who want to buy safe or don't have time to bargain. These 3 chain stores offer large variety of commodities from medium to high quality. Well-known international brands with international warranty.

⑧ ⑨ ⑫ **Gome / Sundan / Suning**		国美、顺电、苏宁
i	• Electrical appliances, entertainment electronics, digital products, household, mobile phones, computers, mp3/mp4 players, etc. • Many outlets throughout Shenzhen • Normally offer free delivery (check conditions with shop)	
♥	Can offer international warranties	
⌛	09am - 10:30pm	
☏	Gome	+86 755 2607 9846 www.gome.com.cn (Chinese)
	Sundan	+86 755 2643 4985 www.sundan.com (Chinese)
	Suning	+86 755 8290 5888 www.cnsuning.com (Chinese)
🚌	MTR: **Huaqiang Lu Station** - 华强路站 Bus: 9, 12, 209, 212	

2nd hand Computers & Accessories 二手电脑

Iɴ ʜᴜᴀɴǫɪᴀɴɢ ʙᴇɪ area there area few places where 2nd hand computers and computers accessories are sold. The best place is Huaqiang Electronics Plaza 华强电子世界 ㉑ on the 4th floor.

Second choice is Saige (SEG) Computer Market 塞格电子市场 ① floors 3 and above.
Next is the Foreign Trade Clothing Market 嘉华外贸服装市场 ⑰ located at the rear left side.

> **!**
> - You might be given one to four weeks to return the product in case of failure. However, <u>examine what you are purchasing very carefully</u> and ask for a receipt.
> - Never buy laptops from the street. These are said to be the latest but actually a software trick will make you believe so, the hardware **is outdated**.

Cʜᴇᴄᴋ ᴛʜᴇ Chinese Corner section at the end of this chapter to learn some Chinese vocabulary when buying computers & electronics.

Mobile Phones & Accessories 手机、手机配件

Tᴏ ᴘᴜʀᴄʜᴀsᴇ ᴍᴏʙɪʟᴇ phones in Huaqiang Bei there are a few places where you can go. At Gome 国美, Suning 苏宁 or Sundan 顺电, you can purchase mobile phones with warranty, even international warranty for some. Prices here are relatively average. For a slightly cheaper bargain, go to either Xieheng 协亨, iTell 易天, or Holpe 恒波. Without doubt, the best deal you can get in China, but without any warranty however, is at Yuanwang Digital City

远望数码城. This mall is packed with small stalls selling any mobile phones you can think of; name it, it will be there. Prices are about 20-30% cheaper than elsewhere. At the basement are mobile phone accessories, first floor are mobiles phones, PDAs, and some gadgets, 2nd and above are the best deals. No English is spoken here, but they understand enough for you to be satisfied. Check out the Chinese brands TCL, Konka, ZTC, etc.

BEST PRICES IN town, and perhaps in China. Yuanwang Digital City 远望数码城 is the place for buying mobile phones of all kinds. This 4-floor building packed with mobile phones retailers offers the best prices in town but does not offer warranties. Check Xieheng 协亨, Holpe 恒波, or iTell 易天 ⑳ to purchase mobile phones with warranty. Yuanwang Digital City is the biggest place in China dealing with mobile phone in Shuihuobusiness 水货.

❻ Yuanwang Digital City		远望数码城
i	Service center for foreign mobile phone merchants: +86 755 8399 8928	
♥	• Shop 2800 on the 2nd floor repairs mobile phones • Shops 1022 & 1559 on the 1st floor repair PDA	
!	Once you leave the shop from which you have purchased your mobile phone, it normally cannot be returned even in case of failure. <u>Examine what you are purchasing very carefully</u> and ask for a receipt, just in case the retailer is willing to help you. When testing the phone you want to purchase, DON'T remove the plastic cover or else the dealer might not be able to return it to its retailer if faulty. Nothing should happen to you, but it's pure loss for them.	
save $	Prices are about 20-30% lower than elsewhere. It is almost impossible to bargain here as this place is normally for wholesale. Prices fluctuate everyday depending on the quantity they sold the day before and the market price. However, if you speak a little Chinese and smile, you might get some discount.	
⧖	10am - 7pm	
☏	www.0101e.com (Chinese)	

深圳购物

XIEHENG 协亨, Holpe 恒波, and iTell 易天 ⑳ are the best places to purchase mobile phones with warranty. Check also Gome 国美, Sundan 顺电 and Suning 苏宁.

⑳ Xieheng, Holpe, iTell 协亨、恒波、易天

✉	There are a few of these shops located along Huaqiang Bei Rd., you can't miss them. Refer to the map pages 70-71.
⏳	9am - 10pm
🚌	MTR: Huaqiang Lu Station - 华强路站 Bus: 9, 12, 209, 212
✆	Xieheng: +86 755 8327 2978 Holpe: +86 755 8399 8866

Don't forget to register at www.szCityGuide.com to report your findings!

Audio-Video & Electronics

音响、电子

Credits 唐筱德

Best place in Huanqiang Bei to buy DVD players, home theaters, HIFI systems, high-end speakers. Specialized in dealing with high-end branded equipment.

7 Wanshang Electronics City		万商电器城
i	Cheaper but relatively lower quality Hi-fi equipment also available at International Electronics Market ③ The layout of this shopping mall is a little confusing. There is one entrance shared with Gome Electronics, and one entrance on the right end side with a banner showing 万商电器城.	
F	1F	Gome Shopping Mall
	2F	Computers and computer accessories, 2nd hand computers on the left side. HI-FI, CD, DVD players, LCD TV screens on the left side of the Mall.
	3F	Software, 2nd hand computers and some computer accessories.
♥	• Tube/Lamp Amplifiers sold at C115 • Tubes/Lamps sold separately at C127 & 3F5 • High-End Hi-fi cables sold at 132 & 152 • Sono equipment available at C142 • Yamaha store at C145 • Do-IT-Yourself Tube/Lamp amplifiers available at 3FB6B, check www.cndi-yshop.com, tel 136 0260 2102	
⧗	9am - 5pm	
☎	+86 755 6163 9998	

Credits 唐晓波

Credits 唐晓波

SHOPPING IN SHENZHEN

www.szCityGuide.com

深圳购物

THE INTERNATIONAL ELECTRONICS Markets (the one along Huaqiang Bei and the one behind Saige/SEG) are said to be foreigners' favorite places to shop for small electronic gadgets. At the mall located along Huaqiang Bei Rd., the products are mainly made in China and reasonably cheap. The mall behind Saige/SEG (picture on the right) has a wider choice for latest devices. Main products are mp3/mp4 players, cameras, mobile phones, TV, video, DVD players, car radio/CD sets, etc, communication equipment and accessories, such as small appliances.

❸ International Electronics Market		国际电子城
F	1F	Mobile phones, Communications, Fax, Security & Monitoring, Walkie-talkies
	2F	Hi-fi, Digital, mp3/mp4, small electronic products, video game players
	3F	Mobile phone accessories wholesale & retail: casing, batteries, chargers, keyboards, ornaments, etc.
⌛	9:30 - 10pm	
🚌	MTR: **Huaqiang Lu Station** - 华强路站 Bus: 9, 12, 209, 212	
✐	www.digitalmarket.net.cn	

CHECK THE Chinese Corner section at the end of this chapter to learn some Chinese vocabulary when buying computers & electronics.

Credits 唐毅德

Credits 唐毅德

GOME, SUNDAN OR Suning is a relatively good alternative to customers who want to buy safe or don't want to bargain. These chain stores offer large variety of commodities from medium to high quality.

	⑧ ⑨ ⑫ **Gome / Sundan / Suning** 国美、顺电、苏宁	
i	• Electrical appliances, entertainment electronics, digital products, households, mobile phones, computers, mp3/mp4 players, etc. • Many outlets in Shenzhen • Normally offers free delivery (check conditions with shop) • Computers are also available but in a rather limited range. Check Saige (SEG) ① and Huaqiang World ⑱ & ㉑ for a wider choice	
♥	• Offer international warranties • Often reported as being the 3 best places to buy TV / LCD TV. Check also International Electronics Market ③ to compare prices	
⌛	9:30 - 10pm	
☏	Gome	+86 755 2607 9846 www.gome.com.cn (Chinese)
	Sundan	+86 755 2643 4985 www.sundan.com (Chinese)
	Suning	+86 755 8290 5888 www.cnsuning.com (Chinese)
🚌	MTR: Huaqiang Lu Station - 华强路站 Bus: 9, 12, 209, 212	

Other Products

其它产品

SPECIALIZING IN SECURITY (picture on the left) and monitoring systems from IR cameras to underwater security systems, car alarms, house tele-protection, etc., this market is the biggest security device market in China. There is another smaller security device market behind the Pacific Protection & Security Market, the products are cheaper but lower in terms of quality.

❷ **The Pacific Protection & Security Market** 太平洋安防通讯市场
♥ For Security products, call Queenie Liu (Speaks very good English, used to dealing with foreigners.) Refer to the map pages 70-71. Shenzhen JIN Technology co., LTD 298B, 2/F, International Electronics City **Huaqiang North Rd.** 华强北国际电子城二楼298B Tel: +86 755 8346 2589, +86 755 8279 8718 Opening hours: 9:30am - 8pm www.jincctv.cn **Product/Services**: CCTV Camera, CCD Camera, Wireless Camera, IP Camera, DVR, DVR Card, Video Card, PTZ Dome Camera, Speed Dome Camera, Mobile DVR, Standalone DVR, Dummy Camera, Hidden Camera, Security Camera, PTZ Camera, Bus DVR, Video Board, DVR Board, Bullets Infrared Camera, CCTV Card, Baby Monitor
⏳ 9:30am - 7pm
🚌 MTR: Huaqiang Lu Station - 华强路站 Bus: 9, 12, 209, 212
✆ www.tpy888.com (Chinese)

Credits 唐秋德

Credits 唐秋德

WATCH CITY OFFERS a wide choice of watches from low to medium quality. Here you can also find bracelets, boxes, pens, jewels, mural clocks, alarm clocks, and all sorts of small tools and measure instruments. There is also a small repair center. For higher quality repair service, go to the Duty Free Jewelry 免税集团珠宝世界, check the women's section next page. When facing Nico New Women's world, walk along Zhenxing Xi Road. It's a couple of blocks away on your right hand side.

!: Examine what you are purchasing very carefully and ask for a receipt.

⑭ **Watch City**	钟表配套市场
i	Floor 1, Block 505, Shangbu Gongyequ, Zhenxingxi Rd., Futian 福田区福田振兴西路上步工业区505栋首层
⏳	9:30am - 6pm
☏	+86 755 8326 6212, 8324 4517
🖱	http://www.zbptsc.com/english/ctc.htm (English)

CHECK OUT THE Chinese Corner section at the end of this chapter to learn some Chinese vocabulary when buying computers & electronics.

SHOPPING IN SHENZHEN

WWW.SZCITYGUIDE.COM

深圳购物

Women & Children at Huaqiang Bei

Children's World	儿童世界
Nico Women's World Fashion Plaza	女人世界名店
MOI Shopping Center	茂业百货
Women's World	女人世界
Foreign Trade Clothing Market	嘉华外贸服装市场
Duty Free Jewelry	免税集团珠宝世界

Credits 唐敬德

SELLING TONS OF things for children: clothing, toys, roller blades, pajamas, hair and jewelry accessories and a very large selection of shoes. Also available are items for babies: cribs, strollers, car seats, walkers and more. Children's World is made up of many small shops under one roof. Each shop sells separately, but you have to pay at central payment booths located throughout the store. After you've paid, bring your receipts back to the shop and collect your merchandise. Don't forget to bargain. Most people don't speak English, but can usually understand enough to give you what you want. There is an indoor playroom and art center for children to use while you shop. The cost for the playroom is 20RMB per hour. Art work is separate, but reasonably priced. Store employees will supervise children while you shop.

⑪ Children's World		儿童世界
i	• Located at the end of Huaqiang Rd., next to Gome. • There is another Children's World branch in Nanshan, a few blocks away from Book City.	
F	1F	Children's clothes
	2F	Children's shoes, maternity clothes
	3F	Toys, stationery, electronics, books, beddings, musical instruments Toilets
⧖	9:30am - 10pm	

深圳购物指南

Credits 唐锐德

NICO WOMEN'S WORLD Fashion Plaza is an upscaled shopping mall selling mid to high quality clothing and fashion accessories. There are 2 Women's Worlds along Huaqiang Bei Rd. One is Nico Women's World, and one is simply Women's World, which sells low to mid quality clothes.

⑬ **Nico Women's World Fashion Plaza**			女人世界名店	
F	1F	Cosmetics, Women's fashion, watches, eye glasses	3F	Beauty salon, women's fashion
	2F	Women's fashion	4F	Clothes, leathers, maternity clothes, pyjamas, wedding dresses, men's clothing
♥	Haagen Daaz next to the main entrance			
☏	+86 755 8323 0188			
⌛	10am - 10pm			
🚌	MTR: Huaqiang Lu Station - 华强路站 Bus: 9, 12, 209, 212			
🖱	www.womensworld.com.cn			

Credits 唐致德

THIS PARTICULAR BRANCH differentiates itself from the others by offering a wider choice of international brands like Chanel, Dior, M.A.C, Mango, Joy&Peace, Staccato, Boss, Clavin Klein, Esprit, Kappa, Hush Puppies, Valentino, etc. MOI (pronounced Maoye in Chinese Mandarin) is targeted to the 20-45 age group, popular styles, and intended for white collars workers and business people.

⑲ **MOI Shopping Center**				茂业百货

i	• There is a 2-storey Starbucks coffee shop located at the ground floor (go upstairs for a quieter space). Refer to the map pages 70-71. • Piano seller, Parson Music, located on the 8th.			

	B1	Supermarket	5F	Men's clothing
	1F	Fashion & cosmetics	6F	Casual wear
F	2F	Young girls	7F	Sport wear
	3F	Women's fashion	8F	Children's wear & shoes
	4F	Beauty & underwear	9F	Furniture & household

ℂ	+86 755 8321 0000
🚌	MTR: Huaqiang Lu Station - 华强路站 Bus: 9, 12, 209, 212
⏳	10am - 11pm

Credits 唐晓德

DO NOT MIX this Women's World and NICO Women's World Fashion Plaza ⑬. This particular Women's World sells mostly Chinese clothing at reasonable prices and rather good quality. Bargaining is highly expected. Check out NICO Women's World ⑬ if you are looking for branded products. Go to the Foreign Clothing Market ⑰ if you are looking for foreign big sizes.

⑯ **Women's World**			女人世界	
i	Women's World is located at the end of Huaqiang Bei Rd., next to Children's World and Gome. Refer to the map pages 70-71.			
F	1F	Bags, umbrellas, hats, cosmetics, etc.	4F	Women's and men's fashion
	2F	Women's underwear & fashion	5F	Beauty and hair
	3F	Women's fashion		
🚌	MTR: Huaqiang Lu Station - 华强路站 Bus: 9, 12, 209, 212			
✆	+86 755 8324 4788			
🖱	www.womensworld.com.cn			

THE FOREIGN TRADE Clothing Market (aka U.S. Market) is a one-floor quasi-open air market place. Located right behind MOI Shopping Center ⑲. Chinese people as well as more and more foreigners prefer this place to shop for clothes rather than Luohu Commercial City as it is cheaper and less crowded. Good quality, big sizes, very good prices. Bargaining is highly expected.

⑰ Foreign Trade Clothing Market　嘉华外贸服装市场

i
- There is a book store selling foreign books in English, Russian, French, Spanish and Japanese languages. Haisan Book Store: 广场大地门口A1铺
  ☏ 135 1099 1260, 136 9218 8130

- A 2nd hand market that sells all kinds of electronics is located on the rear left side of the market.

save $	Bargain down to pay about 50-70% of the asking price.
⧖	10am - 10pm

Credits 唐锐悠

DUTY FREE JEWELRY is a modern, clean and spacious 2-storey building selling jewelry at great quality and reasonable prices. You can have your watch or jewelry repaired or serviced on the second floor.

⑤ **Duty Free Jewelry**		免税集团珠宝世界
F	1F	Diamond, jade, emerald
	2F	Gold, platinum, silver, watches, crystal, pearl
✉	Floor 1-3, Building Xi, Hualianfa Dasha, No. 2006, Huaqiang Bei, Futian 福田区华强北路2006号华联发大厦西座1-3楼	
✆	+86 755 8399 9595	
🚌	MTR: Huaqiang Lu Station - 华强路站 Bus: 9, 12, 209, 212	
⏳	Weekdays: 10am - 10pm Weekends: 9:30am - 10:30pm	

CHECK THE Chinese Corner section at the end of this chapter to learn some Chinese vocabulary when buying for women and children.

深圳购物

Don't forget to register at www.szCityGuide.com
to report your findings!

Shopping along the Metro line, *and beyond...*

TRAVELING ALONG THE MTR line is a good a way to go from shopping places to shopping places in Shenzhen, provided that you don't carry too many bags with you.

At present, the MTR lines 1 and 4 don't serve the whole of Shenzhen, but by 2010, when the lines 2 and 3 open, you should be able to access most of Shenzhen's 6 districts shopping centers via MTR.

For your convenience, we have placed Shenzhen's most popular shopping malls on the map next page, along with some important details such as border crossings, ferry terminal, MTR stations, and airport.

少年宫 Shaonian Gong
市民中心 Shimin Zhongxin

6:30 - 23:00

Huizhan Zhongxin 会展中心

6:30 - 23:00

世界之窗 Shijie Zhichuang
华侨城 Huaqiao Cheng
车公庙 Chegong Miao
侨城东 Qiaocheng Dong
竹子林 Zhuzi Lin
香蜜湖 Xiangmi Hu
购物公园 Gouwu Gongyuan
岗厦 Gangxia
华强路 Huaqiang Lu
科学馆 Kexue Guan
大剧院 Dajuyuan
老街 Laojie
国贸 Guomao
罗湖 Luohu

Fumin 福民

Huanggang 皇岗

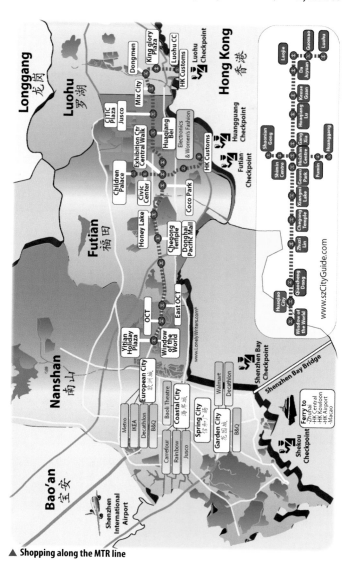

▲ **Shopping along the MTR line**

深圳购物指南

MIXC OR MIX City, in Chinese Mandarin is "Wanxiang" 万象, which literally means: *"all phenomena on earth."* To some extent it is what you will find in MixC shopping Center. This Shopping Mall is for now the largest (and easily the most expensive) shopping mall in Shenzhen. It includes the following: Olympic size indoor Ice Skating Rink, Golden Harvest Cinema movie theater, Ole - high end supermarket with many imported items, Spaghetti House, Starbucks, and Taco Bell (not the fast food variety, but an actual restaurant.) Also here are major brands such as Armani, Hugo Boss, Mont Blanc, etc.

Credits 唐裝德

MixC Shopping Mall	万象城
✉ 1881 Bao'an Rd, Luohu 罗湖区宝安南路1881号	
✆ +86 755 8266 8447	
⌛ 09am - 10pm	
🚌 MTR: Da Juyuan Station, exit C3 大剧院站，C3出口	
🖱 www.mixc.com.cn (English)	

Credits 朱琛

CITIC PLAZA IS another Shopping complex in Shenzhen. It has usual shops, restaurants, Jusco and Seibu the Japanese supercenter. If you crave western stuff, it's here. The plaza also houses a movie theater and several Western restaurants like Pizza Hut, Haagen Daaz, KFC, and Starbucks.

CITIC Plaza   中信广场

✉	Citic Plaza,1093Shennan Road Central, Luohu 罗湖区深南中路1093号中信大厦
⌛	10am - 10pm
🚌	MTR: Kexue Guan Station, exit D - 科学馆站, D出口

DONG HAI PACIFIC Mall is a new 4 level mall and movie theatre, featuring array of restaurants, coffee shops, clothing and other goods. Located In the heart of Donghai 东海 neighborhood on the westside of the Futian district 福田区, just 2 blocks away from the Sam's Club/Cinema complex.

Donghai Pacific Mall   东海购物广场

✉	At the intersection of Xiangmi Hu, Nongyuan Rd. and Lisi Rd., Futian 福田区香蜜湖农园路和红荔西路交会处
🚌	MTR: Chegong Miao Station - 车公庙站 ⌛ 10am - 10pm

深圳购物指南

Credits 林琛

KINGGLORY PLAZA IS a mall along the lines of MixC, high priced. It sas a movie theater as well as the "IN" bar/nightclub and Yellow bar.

King Glory also houses the largest Omega boutique and Solomon store in Shenzhen.

King Glory Plaza	金光华广场
✉	NO.2028,South Renmin Road,Luohu 罗湖区人民南路2028号
✆	+86 755 8222 6435
⧗	8am - 10pm
🚌	MTR: Guo Mao Station, exit A - 国贸站, A出口

CHECK THE Chinese Corner section at the end of this chapter to learn some Chinese vocabulary when buying food.

Credits 唐晓德

Credits 林琛

COCO PARK IS a shopping mega complex located above Gouwu Goongyuan MTR station 购物公园站. You will find here sports clothing, fashion, restaurants, including "Norway Oslo" which has some outdoor seating.

Coco Park	购物公园
✉	**Xinghe COCO park, Fuhua Rd. 3,** Futian 福田区福华三路星河 COCO Park
⌛	**10am – 10pm** **Friday and Saturday until 10:30pm**
🚍	MTR: **Gouwu Gongyuan Station** 购物公园站
🖱	www.cocopark.cn (Chinese)

SHOPPING IN SHENZHEN

www.szCityGuide.com

深圳购物

Credits 林深

CENTRAL WALK IS another shopping complex in Shenzhen. Base tenant is Carrefour, but also has usual shops, restaurants and a cinema. Starbucks and Italian Best Coffee (Illy Coffee), Subway Sandwiches also have opened here. Located one block away from the exhibition centre on Fuhua Road. To get there, take the MTR to Exhibition Centre Station exit B; Central Walk is located only 5 minutes walk from Coco Park.

Central Walk	怡景中心城
✉	Fuhua Rd. 1, Futian (opposite the Exhibition Center) 福田区福华一路 (深圳会展中心对面)
⧗	10am - 10:30pm
🚌	MTR: Huizhan Zhongxin Station, exit B5 会展中心站, B5出口
🖱	www.centralwalk.com (Chinese)

CHECK THE Chinese Corner section at the end of this chapter to learn some Chinese vocabulary when buying food.

Credits 唐晟德

SHENZHEN BOOK CITY is a huge bookstore with a great selection of books, music, movies, and multimedia products. The three-floor book city is the second biggest in the country, it houses more than just books. It also has restaurants, antique shops, convenience stores, art shops, and other shops to satisfy customers' wide range of requirements. Books are divided into six categories: leisure life, music, children's books, social sciences, and business management. The "music" zone has CDs and VCDs on music, films and traditional operas.

For English books, there is Yiwen Bookstore (see above picture). This imported books store is the first imported books store in the city. Yiwen also sells novels and books on film, design and business management, novels, children's books, history, politics, IT, and science books. Books at the store can get quite expensive compared to domestic books. Except for some cheap classic novels, an imported book costs about 10 percent higher than that in the publishing countries. Yet the bookstore does have some books hard to find elsewhere in the city.

Shenzhen Book City	深圳书城
✉	Fuzhong 1 Rd. , Futian 福田区福中一路
☎	+86 755 8289 3888 / Yiwen book store +86 755 2399 2112
🚌	MTR: Shaonian Gong Station - 少年宫站 Bus: 25, 64, 65, 71, 111; get off at Children's Palace Shaonian Gong 少年宫站
🖱	www.szbookmall.com www.szlib.gov.cn/english/main.html

深圳购物指南

Shopping in Nanshan

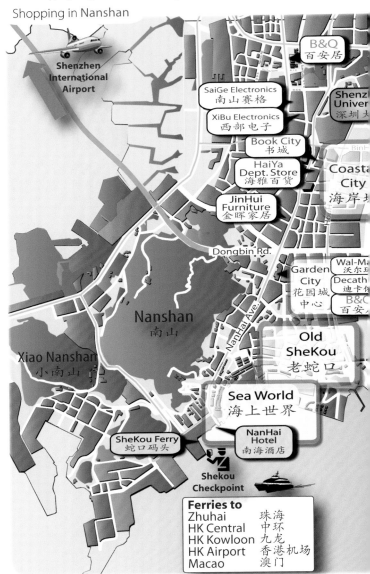

Shenzhen International Airport

B&Q
百安居

SaiGe Electronics
南山赛格

XiBu Electronics
西部电子

Book City
书城

HaiYa Dept. Store
海雅百货

JinHui Furniture
金晖家居

Shenz Univer
深圳大

Coasta City
海岸坡

Dongbin Rd.

Garden City
花园城中心

Wal-Ma
沃尔玛
Decath
迪卡侬
B&Q
百安

NanHai Ave.

Nanshan
南山

Old SheKou
老蛇口

Xiao Nanshan
小南山

Sea World
海上世界

NanHai Hotel
南海酒店

SheKou Ferry
蛇口码头

Shekou Checkpoint

Ferries to
Zhuhai   珠海
HK Central   中环
HK Kowloon   九龙
HK Airport   香港机场
Macao   澳门

深圳购物

SHOPPING IN SHENZHEN

www.szCityGuide.com

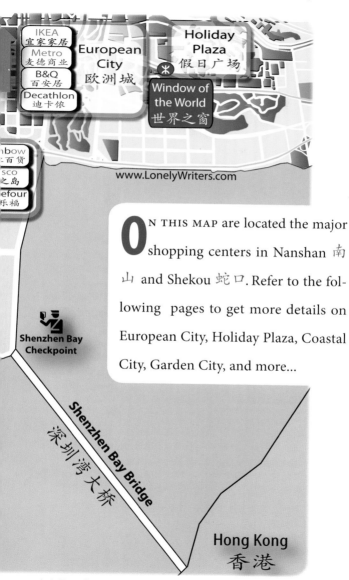

IKEA
宜家家居
Metro
麦德龙商业
B&Q
百安居
Decathlon
迪卡侬

European City
欧洲城

Holiday Plaza
假日广场

Window of the World
世界之窗

bow
百货
sco
之岛
efour
乐福

www.LonelyWriters.com

Shenzhen Bay Checkpoint

ON THIS MAP are located the major shopping centers in Nanshan 南山 and Shekou 蛇口. Refer to the following pages to get more details on European City, Holiday Plaza, Coastal City, Garden City, and more...

Shenzhen Bay Bridge
深圳湾大桥

Hong Kong
香港

深圳购物 **SHOPPING IN SHENZHEN**

www.szCityGuide.com

深圳购物

COASTAL CITY IS an up market shopping center with more than 240 stores. The retail giants make the Houhai area one of the three most important shopping destinations in Shenzhen, along with Dongmen and Huaqiang Bei. Coastal City not only includes a theatre, an exhibition center, museums, entertainment, dining, cultural and sports facilities, shopping malls, but also restaurants featuring cuisine of different styles. Golden Harvest has opened South China's largest movie screen in the mall, which also has Shenzhen's first ice hockey club. Right opposite to Coastal City is Poly Cultural Center, an upscale mall housing Rainbow Department Store and Carrefour supermarket. The four-storey Rainbow Department Store, is the local retail chain's first mall targeting high-end customers. The Japanese Jusco is also here.

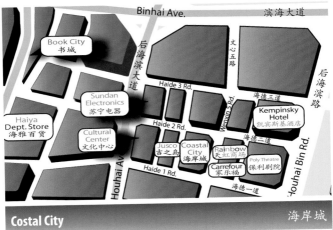

Costal City   海岸城

✉	Crossroad between Wenxin No.5 road and Haide No.1 avenue, Nanshan (Beside Kempinski Hotel, refer to the Coastal City map above) 南山区文心五路与海德一道交汇处保利文化广场(凯宾斯基酒店旁)
🚌	Bus: 229, J1, 39, 72, 121, 109, 334, 51, 322, 19, 31, 37, 355, , 76, 80, 231, 305, 322, 353, 382 MTR: No direct line, go to Window of the World Station - 世界之窗站 and take one of the buses mentioned above.

Credits 林琛

Credits 唐毅德

深圳购物

SHOPPING IN SHENZHEN

www.szCityGuide.com

YITIAN HOLIDAY PLAZA is a 6-start hotel and shopping plaza combined. It is located in the OCT area, opposite Window of the World. Its design is inspired by a luxury city cruise boat.

Fashion

Yitian Holiday Plaza targets high-level consumers. 40% of the brands are new to Shenzhen, including well-known international brands like ARMANI COLLEZIONI, HUGO BOSS, CERRUTI 1881, etc. COLLEZIONI (under the brand ARMANI.) The ZARA store is the first in southern China. The beauty cosmetic chain SEPHORA 丝芙兰 with other famous world brands are opening outlets in Yitian.

Entertainment

- Membership club luxury theatre 中影嘉禾影院, zhongying jiahe yingyuan. You can sit or lie down in the theatre's luxury seats. It provides comprehensive VIP services, bringing a world-class movie experience to Shenzhen. This theatre introduces the membership club concept, screening the members' favorite movies. There will be movie activities like meeting the stars, film premieres, etc.
- "Kasa bulanka" movie culture bar

"卡萨布兰卡" 电影文化酒吧 Morocco decoration style. Besides the movies, members can enjoy the relaxed environment of the movie bar.

- All champions skating pool China's first spectator skating rink. Planned by China's famous "gymnastics prince" Li Ning, and run by International skating champions, the skating rink plans to hire famous sport stars to coach. It is the first spectator skating rink in China. Surrounded by 5 floors of the shopping mall, skaters will feel like a performer on the stage.

Food

The biggest buffet in Southern China 四海一家 Sihai Yijia, provides a full range of choice. You can combine the flavours of the world during a meal: Italian, French, Japanese and Korean food are served alongside South East Asian snacks, Brazilian BBQ, Indian curry and Chinese banquet-style cuisine.

Star Bar

There is a sea view terrace bar, from which, in the daytime, you can enjoy the natural views of Overseas Town and Shenzhen Bay. In the evening you can see the fireworks from Window of the World.

Holiday Plaza 假日广场

✉	Opposite Window of the World, OCT, Nanshan 南山区世界之窗对面
☏	Opening in August 2008
⌐	www.ytholidayplaza.com
🚌	MTR: Window of the World Station - 世界之窗站

Located in Nanshan area, along Nanshan Avenue, Spring City Plaza is a 4-floor department store that is targeted to be a smaller version of Huaqiang Bei, the famous electronics district. Spring City Plaza will house electronics and computer stores, as well as fashion stores, and restaurants. Opening in Agust 2008

Spring City Plaza 信和广场

✉	Nanshan Avenue, Nanshan. 南山区南山大道
☏	Opening in August 2008
🚌	Bus: 113, 70 MTR: No direct line

CHECK THE Chinese Corner section at the end of this chapter to learn some Chinese vocabulary when shopping.

深圳购物

SHOPPING IN SHENZHEN

www.szCityGuide.com

Credits: 唐晓德

GARDEN CITY IS located in Nanshan, along Nanshan Avenue. Besides the MCL cinema, Garden City houses well-known stores such as Wal-Mart, Decathlon sports, B&Q, Zijincheng department store, and Chow Tai Fook jewelry. Many restaurants such as Genryoku Sushi, Papa John's, and many boutiques are also here.

Garden City				花园城中心
F	B1	Carpark Note: carpark entrance located behind the shopping mall	3F	Underwear, Adidas bags and sportswear, large space of cosmetics ♥ Triumph underwear, Bodum tea pots# 309, Bossini clothes #309, some cosmetics brands, as Jeanne Piaubert, l'Oreal, Lierac.
	1F	Jewelry, shoes, cosmetics ♥ Geox shoes, Cacharel for baby, Mango. Apple store.	4F	Restaurants, boutiques ♥ Victory restaurant – Chinese - . Comvita New Zealand health care products.
	2F	Large space of cosmetics, shoes, bags, sportswear ♥ Wrangler, Levis, Nike	5F	MCL Cinema, 700 seats, 5 individual cinemas
✉		Nanshan Avenue, Nanshan 区南区花园城南山区南海大道		
🚌		MTR: No direct line. Bus: 113, 70; get off at Wal-mart Station - 沃尔玛站		

Credits 唐联德

EUROPEAN CITY HOUSES outlets of four European retailing giants, the Swedish furniture retail chain Ikea, the British home improvement tools and supplies retailer B&Q, the German supermarket chain Metro and the French sports equipment manufacturer Decathlon. Located near the intersection of North Ring Road, Shahe Road East and the Guangzhou-Shenzhen Expressway.

European City 欧洲城

 8188 Beihuan Rd., at the junction between Beihuan Ave. and Xibei Corner, Nanshan
南山区北环大道8188号(沙河东路北环大道交界西北角)

i ♥ The Metro store located in European City has a large choice of wine at very reasonable prices, a refrigerated room full of fresh organic meat from Mongolia: beef tenderloin, lamb, pork, Mc Cormick spices.
♥ This particular IKEA is the first store in Shenzhen.

Credits 唐联德

Credits 唐联德

Furniture and Home Décor

WITH THE INCREASE of interest from the Chinese people for modern western type of furniture and the growing number of expatriates in Shenzhen, more and more choices are offered to you when buying furniture in Shenzhen. Ikea has recently opened its first store in Nanshan district at European City. B&Q runs a few malls throughout Shenzhen, Hoba is one of expats' favorite places to buy furniture.

Also, just like there is the Huaqiang Bei area for electronics, Luohu CC and Dongmen for fashion, there is the Four Dragons for home décor, and Sungang area for furniture.

Four Dragons Home, also known as the Light Industrial Products City, is the ideal place to shop for home décor in Shenzhen. There are hundreds of shops gathered in two 7-storey malls. You will find a great selection of lamps, artificial plants, furniture, ceramics, art, and much more. You should try to bargain in all shops. Quality ranges from medium to high. Surrounding Four Dragons are shops selling similar merchandise with new places opening all the time, so venture out if you have time or money left. Delivery can be arranged for large pieces.

Home Décor

Credits 唐张德

Four Dragons Home		艺展中心
F	Phase I	Home ornament, craft work, classical furniture, chinaware & glassware, flower & floriculture, home layout professional designers.
	Phase II	Home ornament show rooms, lifestyle and leisure showrooms, recreation & coffee house.

✉	811, 812, 814 Meiyuan Rd., Sungang Wuliu Area 罗湖区笋岗物流区梅园路811,812,814号
☏	+86 755 8249 7912
🚌	Bus: 209, 212, 218, 303, 322, 323, 333, 336, 453, 462 Get off at Meiyuanlu 梅园路
⌛	9:30am - 7pm
🖱	www.yizhanzx.com

Home Furnishings

Credits 林深

SUNGANG FURNITURE CITY is a well known 4-storey mall to buy furniture in Shenzhen. Around Sungang Furniture City you'll find many other furniture malls. Quality ranges from mid to high. Prices are reasonable. You will also find some 2nd hand furniture shops around.

Sungang Furniture City   笋岗香江家具城

✉	Floors 1-4, Rencai Dashichang, Bao'an Bei Rd. 罗湖区宝安北路人才大市场1-4楼
☏	+86 755 8241 0856
🚌	Bus: 23, 24, 201, 18, 474, 447, 448; get off at Bao'an Bei Rd. intersection 宝安 北路口站
⌛	9am - 10:30pm

FOUNDED IN 1998, HOBA is a well-known furnishings chain enterprise in China. It is headed in Shenzhen and operates under two retail brands: HOBA Home Furnishings, METEN Living Design. HOBA has 20 furnishing chain stores nationwide, with 4 in Shenzhen.

Website: www.hoba.com.cn

HOBA Home Furnishings 好百年家居

Location 1 - Luohu district

F1-4 Rencai Shichang, Bao'an Bei Rd.
Tel: +86 755 8244 9538
罗湖区宝安北路人才大市场1-4楼
Mon-Thu : 9am - 9pm, Fri-Sun: 9am - 9:30pm

Location 2 - Futian district - Note: locations 2 & 3 are not far apart

HOBA Home Furnishings Plaza, No.3006, Caitian Road, Futian
Tel: +86 755 8292 4537
福田区彩田路3006号
Mon-Thu : 9am - 9pm, Fri-Sun: 9am - 9:30pm

Location 3 - Futian district - Note: locations 2 & 3 are not far apart

1-4F, Skirt Building, Caitian Mingyuan, No.3010, Caitian Road, Futian
Tel: +86 755 8291 1673
福田区彩田南路3010号彩天名苑裙楼1-4楼
Bus:4,14,35,56; get off at Caifu Dasha 彩福大厦
Mon-Thu: 9am - 9pm, Fri-Sun: 9am - 9:30pm

Location 4 - Bao'an district

HOBA Home Furnishings Plaza, Qianjin Road No.1, 25th Area, Bao'an.
Tel: +86 755 2785 6818
宝安25区前进一路
Bus:74,18,33,63; get off at Rencai Shichang 人才市场
Mon-Thu : 9am - 9pm, Fri-Sun: 9am - 9:30pm

Home Furnishings & DIY

THE BRITAIN-BASED B&Q has different locations in Shenzhen. B&Q offers a warehouse retailing approach to the home improvement and home furnishings market. Website: www.bnq.com.cn

B&Q	百安居

Location 1 - Luohu district

4008 Bao'an Bei Rd.
罗湖区宝安北路4008号（泥岗路口）
Tel: +86 755 2593 7788
Bus: 23,24,201,18; get off at Ban'anbei Lukou 宝安北路口   9am - 10pm

Locations 2, 3 & 4 - Nanshan district

Naihai Ave., as part of Garden City, next to Wal-mart
南山区蛇口南海大道与工业八路交汇处东北角
Tel: +86 755 2680 6088
Bus: K113, 113, 328, K204; get off at Wal-mart 蛇口沃尔玛   9am - 10pm

3028 Nanshan Ave., at the intersection of Nanshan Ave. and Shennan Ave.
南山区南山大道3028号（南山大道与深南大道交界处）
Tel: +86 755 8612 1666
Bus: 204, 210, 320, 462, 483, 465, 456
Get off at Nantou Gucheng 南头古城   9am - 10pm

As part of European City (南山区欧洲城), check next page.

Location 5 - Futian district

1-2F, Yunsong Dasha, Chegong Miao
福田区车公庙云松大厦1-2层(滨河大道与泰然九路交汇处)
Tel: +86 755 33366611
Bus: 26, 28, 34, 222, 229, 231, K103, 215, K105, K204; get off at Xiasha 下沙
9am - 10pm

Location 6 - Longgang district

18 Longping Xi Rd., at the intersection of Longping Xi Rd. and Longcheng Zhong Rd.
龙岗区龙平西路和龙城中路交汇处（龙平西路18号）
Tel: +86 7553383 2788
Bus: 361, 309, 870   9am - 9pm

Credits 想就绪

Eof four European retailing giants, the Swedish furniture retail chain Ikea, the British home improvement tools and supplies retailer B&Q, the German supermarket chain Metro and the French sports equipment manufacturer Decathlon. Located near the intersection of North Ring Road, Shahe Road East and the Guangzhou-Shenzhen Expressway.

Ikea	宜家家居

 8188 Beihuan Rd., at the junction between Beihuan Ave. and Xibei Corner, Nanshan
南山区北环大道8188号(沙河东路北环大道交界西北角)
环大道的北边, 沙河东路的西边

Kitchen equipment

INDUSTRIAL QUALITY ITEMS for cooking, baking and serving. Specialized in stainless steel dish ware, ceramic dish ware, gold and silver plated tableware, glass vessel, plastic article, food machinery, refrigeration equipment, cleaning article, hotel furniture, guest house decoration, dish ware for buffet dinner, electric kitchen equipment, hall necessity, etc.

Huibao Kitchen Equipment	惠宝厨具

Huibao Kitchen Equipment 惠宝厨具

✉	**Huibao Bld, Qianjin 1 Rd, 26 Baoan District** 宝安区26前进一路 惠宝厨具大厦
⌛	10am - 7pm
☎	+86 755 2781 5699
🖱	www.huibaochuju.com

CAQ KITCHEN EQUIP-MENT is a 4-floor kitchen equipment store located opposite Dongmen Fabric Market, selling mostly to hotels and restaurants, but also to private households. Fixed prices, good quality.

Credits 林琛

CAQ Kitchen Equipment 厨安居

F	1F	Large choice of cooking ceramic pots.	3F	Hotel and Restaurant equipment, Kitchen *Aid Classic*
	2F	Kitchen equipment : Coffee machines, Blenders, Juice Blenders. Indoor/outdoor thermometer, plain plates or Chinese colored style, Chine *Bone White* porcelain.	4F	Pastry pans Plastic containers.

✉	2163 Hubei Rd., Dongmen, Luohu 罗湖区东门湖贝路2163号
⌛	10am - 7pm
☎	+86 755 8883 8182
🖱	www.caq.cc (Chinese) / caqsky@163.com

Stationery Malls

THE LUOHU STATIONERY Malls are two buildings side by side. There are many shops under one roof, all operating independently. There are many stationery stores as well as shops selling everything from toys and party favors, hair accessories to artificial flowers.

	Luohu Stationery Malls 笋岗文具玩具批发市场
✉	Sungang Wenju Wanju Pifa Shichang. 3, Bao'an Bei Rd., Luohu 罗湖区宝安贝路3号
☎	+86 755 8205 3293
🚌	Bus: 23, 24, 201, 18, 474, 447, 448. Get off at Bao'an Bei Rd. intersection 宝安北路口站
⏳	9am - 7:30pm

THIS STATIONERY MALL is located in Futian. It is equivalent to the above, i.e. there are many shops under one roof, all operating independently. There are many stationery stores as well as shops selling everything from toys and party favors, hair accessories to artificial flowers.

	Futian Stationery Mall 福民文具玩具礼品批发市场
✉	Fumin Wenju Wanju Lipin Pifa Shichang. 236 Fumin Rd., Futian 福田区福民路236号
☎	+86 755 8357 5222
🚌	Bus: 28, 202, 52, 203, 413 MTR: Fumin Station - 福民站
⏳	9am - 7pm

Jewel Shopping Streets

THERE ARE TWO large shopping malls in Shenzhen where you can shop for jewels. There, you will find gold, platinum, silver, jade, pearls, diamonds, jewelry repair centers, and manufacturing tools. They are both international jewelry centres, with more than 100 shops and 27 from overseas.

Note: Since the below locations mainly do wholesale, it can be difficult to bargain in retail trade.

Jewel Shopping Streets

Location 1 - 水贝国际珠宝交易中心 - Luohu district	
i	Guoji (International) Shuibei Zhubao jiaoyi Zhongxin has also many shops around that area, i.e. furniture, lamps, etc.
✉	1, Tianbei 4 Rd., Luohu 罗湖区田贝四路 No.1号
☎	+86 755 2563 9919
🚌	Bus: 1,33,57,63 Get off at Tianbei Silu 田贝四路
⌛	9am - 6pm
Location 2 - 东门水贝珠宝 - Dongmen, Luohu district	
i	Dongmen Shuibei Zhubao 东门水贝珠宝 is the biggest retail centre in Shenzhen. This particular place is located in the center of Dongmen area, next to the Dongmen footbridge. Refer to the Dongmen section of this book to know about great shopping places in Dongmen.
✉	2F, Hongji Donggang Building, Dongmen Zhong Rd. 东门中路鸿基东港大厦2楼
☎	+86 755 82358989
🚌	Bus: 1, 3 ,5, 103 MTR: Laojie Station - 老街站
⌛	10am - 10pm
🖱	www.sb-jewelry.com

深圳购物 · SHOPPING IN SHENZHEN · www.szCityGuide.com

Shopping in Zhuhai, Antiques in Zhongshan

Zhuhai

COMPARED WITH ITS "twin city", Shenzhen, Zhuhai 珠海, on the south bank of the Pearl River Estuary seems relatively peaceful and sedate. For this reason it is a pleasant place for visitors. Originally three or four small fishing villages, Zhuhai has grown into a clean, modern city with good hotels and restaurants. Seafood is a particular favorite of visitors to Zhuhai, with restaurants ranging from small businesses which overflow into the streets after work, along the back streets of Xiangzhou, around the fish market, to large bright, noisy places such as Fisherman's Wharf 渔人码头 (Yuren Matou.) Since few restaurants have English menus pointing at your chosen fish swimming in a tank or bucket is necessary. Western food is available in the major hotels but there are no Starbucks. The number one scenic attraction of Zhuhai is the statue of the fisher girl, located on Lovers' Road just north of Jiuzhou Port 九州码头. There are pleasant walks in the nearby parks. The statue can be reached by the 9 or 99 bus routes or by the red 02 sightseeing bus. Little Yeli (wild fox) Island 野狸岛 100 metres off the shore at Xiangzhou 香州 has recently been extensively developed as a park. You can walk around the island in an hour or two or for double the fun hire a tandem bike. Shopping in Zhuhai cannot compete with Shenzhen for variety but the underground Gongbei Port Plaza 拱北口岸广场 offers bargains galore in clothes, shoes, handbags and outdoor sporting equipment. In addition there are enough nail & massage shops to ensure that shoppers have a relaxing day. Immediately north of the Plaza is Lianhua Lu 莲花路 (Lotus Street) which is an attractive pedestrian precinct lined with small kiosks serving hot and cold drinks. Mango smoothies are my favorites on a hot day. The Gongbei border crossing to Macau 澳门 is one of the busiest in China. The northern end of Shuiwan Street is known to the local expatriates as "Bar Street". At night this is a lively place with numerous outdoor bars & karaoke joints. Commercial attractions in Zhuhai include the New Yuan Ming Palace, numerous hot springs resorts and several golf courses.

Transport notes: Zhuhai can be reached by express buses which run frequently from Luohu or by ferry from Shekou. Buses take two to two & a half hours, whereas the ferry takes 1 hour.

Zhongshan Antique City
Huacai Antique City 华财古玩城

THESE ARE GENUINE antiques – we can make them any size you like!"

These words sum up the remarkable business that is the trade in antiques. To be fair, many of the businesses in the Huacai Antique City do not pretend to sell antiques. Instead you can chose from a dazzling array of well-made reproduction furniture or objects-d'arts ranging from hand-painted jewelry boxes to large, ornate armoires. If you fancy a TV cabinet, a novel CD cabinet or a chopstick box you'll find dozens to choose from. Inside the central building you will also find paintings in many styles as well as porcelain. Outside there are small stores selling garden statuary, carved screens and large wooden doors. Many are reputed to be antiques but more often they have been made from recycled timber and even buried in the ground for a while to acquire that patina of age.

Huacai Antique City is located in Guher village 孤儿, Zhongshan City 中山市. Many of the vendors have websites and on-line catalogues.

Note on Antiques: China's government passed a law in May 2007 banning the export of antiques from before 1911. It is now illegal to purchase antiques from before 1911 and take them out of China. Even antiques bought in proper auctions cannot be taken out of China.

■ Brought to you by
Victoria Steven
UIC

Getting to Zhuhai by bus

From Luohu: 深圳侨社 → 珠海
Shenzhen Qiaoshe → Zhuhai
Time: 7am-9pm, every 15 mins
Price: 85RMB

From Bao'an: 宝安汽车站 → 珠海
Bao An bus station → Zhuhai
Time: 7:15am-6:45pm
Price: 75RMB

From Futian: 福田客运站 → 珠海
Futian Keyun Zhan → Zhuhai
Time: 7:20am-8:20pm, every 15mins
Price: 85RMB

Getting to Zhongshan by bus

From Luohu: 银湖汽车站 → 中山
Yinhu bus station → Zhongshan
Time: 8:10am-1:30pm (2 shuttles/day)
Price: 85RMB

From Bao'an: 宝安汽车站 → 中山
Bao'an bus station → Zhongshan
Time: first 7:40am-7pm
Price: 65RMB

Shopping in Dongguan, Houjie, and Humen

ORIGINALLY DEVELOPED BY the Municipal Government, Dongguan 东莞, our neighbor city has an excellent geographic location, good investment policy, convenient transportation, labor resources, and governmental support on tax, entry & exit. All of these are the reasons why Dongguan city has gained various overseas investors' favor, and it has been "The Place" of many furniture and electronic enterprises to invest. The entry of Hong Kong and Taiwan enterprises not only brought in large investment, but also advanced production technology, equipment and expert management. Furthermore, it also brought in fashionable products design, valuable information channel, modern furniture designs and internationally-known furniture brands. Among other things, Dongguan has been the "promised land" for other industries such as garment and leather. The rapid developments have given way into the city being further developed as townships specializing in different fields.

The township of Houjie is known as the Capital of Furniture in China.

This town is turned from a rural village into an industrialized township following the massive influx of Taiwanese and Hong Kong people in the 1980's. In Houjie 厚街, you can find lots of furniture manufacturers offering contemporary to traditional Chinese designs, from office & bedroom furniture to commercial use. The "furniture street' extends beyond 5 km and the town boasts of more than 400 furniture factories. These factories are conveniently supported by the bi-annual (March and September) International Famous Furniture Fair held in Dongguan Exhibition Center.

For those who are interested in opening their own clothing store, you need to head to Humen 虎门 town. This township is "The place to go for Clothes". Many garment factories are scattered in the area, however, most of them have stores set up in the Fumin Garment district shopping centers. There are several buildings in this shopping Mecca, each building houses many little shops specifically catered to wholesalers. If you plan on buying only a few pieces you'll find that the shops also do retail, however at an inflated rate. It is still a great bargain compared to what you can find in Shenzhen. If garment materials are what you need instead of the finished clothes, head to the International Fabric Market 国际布料广场 Guoji Buliao Guangchang. It is located about 15RMB away (by taxi) from Fumin garment district. Here you will find ribbons to leather, textiles of all patterns and textures as well as real fur (all located on the 2nd floor).

For leather goods, be it for sofa or shoes, the factories are spread out in many townships within Dongguan, Liaobu town, Qishi town, Tangxia town and Chang 'An town. You can find anything made from leather made in these townships, from watch bands to handbags, leather sport shoes to briefcases, as well as furniture. Unlike Humen town which also caters to retail shoppers, you will not be able to find shops selling leather goods. Most companies have customers' samples in their showrooms within the factories but not for sale.

If you still would like to score some shopping in Dongguan, a good place to buy leather goods and other fake leather items is the Wal-Mart shopping center in the heart of Dongguan city center. Wal-Mart takes the space of the first floor, as you go up to the second floor you'll find many shops selling leather goods as well as DVDs, Music CDs and Software programs. This is Dongguan city's version of Luohu Commercial City. However, unlike Luohu Commercial City, the prices at this shopping plaza are not marked at 300-400% of the fair retail price, therefore, you don't need to bargain at 50-75% off of their suggested price. It is a smaller-size shopping mall, with many beauty shops and tattoo parlors located on the third floor.

■ Brought to you by
Shierley Koval
www.ShenzhenSouvenir.com

Getting to Dongguan by bus

银湖汽车站 → 东莞汽车站
Yinhu bus station → Dongguan bus station
Timetable: 7:30am-8:00pm, every 15mins)
Price: 45RMB

福田客运站 → 东莞汽车站
Futian Keyun Zhan → Dongguan bus station
Timetable: 6:30am-7:20pm, every 30mins
Price: 45RMB

罗湖汽车站 → 东莞汽车站
Luohu Bus Station → Dongguan bus station
Timetable: 7:00am-8:30pm, every 15mins
Price: 50RMB

(南山)南新天桥 → 东莞汽车站
(Nanshan) Nanxin Tianqiao → Dongguan bus station
Timetable: 6:50am-7:45pm, every 30mins
Price: 40RMB

世界之窗 → 东莞汽车站
Window of the world → Dongguan bus station
Timetable: 7:25am-7:05pm, every 45mins a shuttle

福田客运站 → 东莞厚街
Futian Keyun Zhan → Dongguan Houjie
Timetable: 7:00am-6:40pm, every 30mins
Price: 35RMB

罗湖汽车站 → 东莞厚街
Luohu Bus Station → Dongguan Houjie
Timetable: 7:30am-9:00pm, every 30mins
Price: 45RMB

Getting to Dongguan by Train

深圳罗湖火车站 → 东莞火车站
Luohu train station → Dongguan train station
Timetable: 6:20am, 10:45pm
Price:first class 45 yuan, economic class 40RMB

罗湖汽车站 → 虎门
Luohu Bus Station → Humen
Timetable: 7:00am, 9:40pm
Price: 42yuan

Getting to Humen by bus

福田客运站 → 虎门
Futian Keyun Zhan → Humen
Timetable: 6:30am-6:45pm every 30mins
Price: 30yuan

(南山)南新天桥 → 虎门
(Nanshan) Nanxin Tianqiao → Humen
Timetable: 6:50am-7:10pm every 20mins
Price: 30yuan

世界之窗 → 虎门
Window of the world → Humen
Timetable: 6:40am-7:00pm every 50mins
Price: 30yuan

Getting to Hujie from Humen

Humen and Houjie are both in Dongguan, at one station away from Humen.
Bus: 107,112B,112,112c,113,115

Getting to Hujie from Dongguan

From Dongguan bus station, it's 2 stations away
From Shiqiche Zongzhan 市汽车总站 118A/118/113/112(/107 to Hujie 厚街

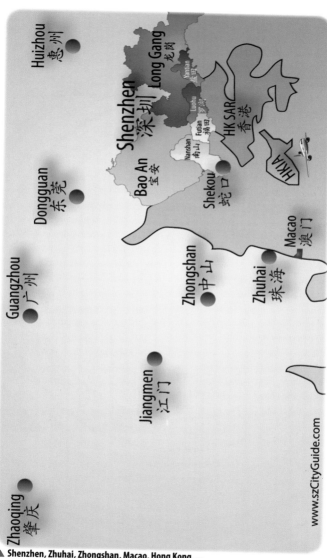

Huizhou
惠州

Shenzhen
深圳

Long Gang
龙岗

Yantian
盐田

Luohu
罗湖

HK SAR
香港

Nanshan
南山

Futian
福田

HKIA

Dongguan
东莞

Bao An
宝安

Shekou
蛇口

Macao
澳门

Guangzhou
广州

Zhongshan
中山

Zhuhai
珠海

Jiangmen
江门

www.szCityGuide.com

Zhaoqing
肇庆

▲ **Shenzhen, Zhuhai, Zhongshan, Macao, Hong Kong, ...**

SHOPPING IN SHENZHEN

深圳购物

Shenzhen Souvenir line

Shenzhen-Souvenir line is here to offer an original selection of things you can bring back in your suitcase. Items we sell are meant to be rolled, easily stored and won't take much space. Come check it out at www.shenzhensouvenir.com to take a peek at Shenzhen-Souvenir styles.

HOW MANY TIMES have you entertained friends, family and business associates from abroad who need to buy souvenirs to bring home for their loved (and not-so-loved) ones?

Well… if you are wondering what souvenir you can buy in a city that is this young, we might be able to give you what you need.

The products
The first collection includes kid and adult T-shirts in different styles and colors, including hoodies; hats and reusable grocery bags.

The idea behind the line is to create a Shenzhen/Chinese-inspired casual wear aimed at foreigners and some locals. Shenzhen-Souvenir line is also into event planning and party-in-a-box.

Come check it out at Seaworld Shekou, in front of Grissini Restaurant. Other locations will follow shortly!

■ Sheirley Koval
www.ShenzhenSouvenir.com

Tracy's Chinese Corner

Key shopping phrases	**129**
Dealing with money	**129**
Dealing with numbers	**130**
Vocabulary	**131**
Arts	**131**
Art	131
Instruments	131
Music	131
Babies	**131**
Books	**131**
Clothing	**132**
Cosmetics	**132**
Electronics	**133**
Apple	136
Digital	135
Games	134
Hardware	133
Hi-fi / Audio Video	135
Mobile phones	135
Networking	134
PC's	133
PDAs & Accessories	133
Software	134
Fabric	**136**
Flowers	**136**
Food & Drink	**136**
Alcohols	136
At the market	137
Basic food	138
Breads & Pastries	138
Fruits	139
Vegetable	139

Furniture	139
Bathroom	139
Bedroom	140
Cups & Glasses	140
Lights & Lamps	143
Living room	140
Kitchen	141
Material	141
Outdoor Furniture	141
Utensils	142
Others	142
Jewelry	**142**
Material	142
Shapes	142
Stones	142
Kids	**143**
Pets	**143**
Pharmacy	**143**
Stationery	**143**
Study	**141**
Tea	**141**
Tailor	**144**
Sizes	144

Key shopping phrases

I want to buy _____ .
我想买_____ . Wǒ xiǎng mǎi_____ .

Excuse me, where can I buy_____ .?
请问哪里可以买 _____? Qǐngwèn nǎlǐ kěyǐ mǎi_____?

May I have a look?
我可以看看吗? Wǒ kěyǐ kànkàn ma?

Do you have any larger /smaller one?
有大/小点的吗? Yǒu dà/xiǎo diǎn de ma?

Do you have a new one?
有新的吗? Yǒu xīn de ma?

I don't like it.
我不喜欢. Wǒ bù xǐhuān.

OK, I'll take it.
要这个. Yào zhègè.

Can I use credit card?
可以刷卡吗? Kěyǐ shuākǎ ma?

I'm just looking.
我看看而已. Wǒ kànkan éryǐ.

Can I have a receipt?
可以给张发票吗? Kěyǐ gěi zhāng fāpiào ma?

Dealing with money

Money 钱 Qián
To pay 付 Fù
Cash 现金 Xiànjīn
Credit Card 信用卡 Xìnyòngkǎ

How much is this?
这个多少钱? Zhègè duōshǎo qián?

That's too expensive!
太贵了! Tài guì le!

What's the last price?
实价多少? Shíjià duōshǎo?

How much discount?
打多少折? Dǎ duōshǎo zhé?

Would you take _____?
_____元可以吗? _____ yuán kěyǐ ma?

Expensive Guì 贵
Cheap 便宜 Piányi

Dealing with numbers

Numbers 数字 shùzì

0	零	líng	18	十八	shí-bā
1	一	yī	19	十九	shí-jiǔ
2	二	èr	20	二十	èr-shí
3	三	sān	21	二十一	èr-shí-yī
4	四	sì	22	二十二	èr-shí-èr
5	五	wǔ	23	二十三	èr-shí-sān
6	六	liù	30	三十	sān-shí
7	七	qī	40	四十	sì-shí
8	八	bā	50	五十	wǔ-shí
9	九	jiǔ	60	六十	liù-shí
10	十	shí	70	七十	qī-shí
11	十一	shí-yī	80	八十	bā-shí
12	十二	shí-èr	90	九十	jiǔ-shí
13	十三	shí-sān	100	一百	yī-bǎi
14	十四	shí-sì	1,000	一千	yī-qiān
15	十五	shí-wǔ	10,000	一万	yī-wàn
16	十六	shí-liù	100,000	十万	shí-wàn
17	十七	shí-qī	1,000,000	一百万	yī-bǎi-wàn

深圳购物

Vocabulary

English	Chinese	Pinyin
Arts		
Art	艺术	yì shù
Calligraphy	书法	shūfǎ
Carving	雕刻	diāokè
Chinese painting	中国画	zhōngguó huà
Dancing	舞蹈	wǔdǎo
Handicraft	手工艺品	shǒugōngyì pǐn
Painting	画画	huàhuà
Paper cut	剪纸	jiǎnzhǐ
Photography	摄影	shèyǐng
Sculpture	雕塑	diāosù
Music		
Music	音乐	yīnyuè
Jazz	爵士	juéshì
Classical	古典	gǔdiǎn
New Age	新世纪	xīnshì jì
Pop	流行	liúxíng
Rock	摇滚	yáogǔn
Instruments		
Instrument	乐器	yuèqì
Accordion	手风琴	shǒufēngqín
Acoustic guitar	原声吉他	yuánshēng jítā
Amplifier	扩音器	kuòyīn qì
Bass guitar	低音电吉他	dīyīn diànjítā
Chinese zither	古筝	gǔzhēng
Clarinet	单簧管	dānhuáng guǎn
Electric guitar	电吉他	diànjítā
Flute	长笛	chángdí
Piano	钢琴	gāngqín
Trumpet	喇叭	lǎbā
Violin	小提琴	xiǎotíqín
Babies		
For the baby	婴儿用品	yīng'ér yòngpǐn
Baby carriage	婴儿车	yīng'ér chē
Baby powder	爽身粉	shuǎngshēnfěn
Bib	围兜	wéidōu
Cradle	摇篮	yáolán
Diaper	尿片	niàopiàn
Feeding bottle	奶瓶	nǎipíng
Milk powder	奶粉	nǎifěn
Books		
Book	书	shū

Cooking book	烹饪书	pēngrèn shū
Dictionary	词典	cídiǎn
Encyclopedia	百科全书	bǎikēquánshū
Novel	小说	xiǎoshuō
Gardening	园艺	yuányì
Literature	文学	wénxué
Science	科学	kēxué
Sport	体育	tǐyù
Text book	课本	kèběn
Thriller	惊险	jīngxiǎn
Traveling	旅游	lǚyóu

Clothing

Bra	文胸	wénxiōng
T-shirt	T-恤	tīxù
Ceremonial robe	礼服	lǐfú
Dress	裙子	qúnzi
Jeans	牛仔裤	niúzǎikù
Pants	裤子	kùzi
Pyjamas	睡衣	shuìyī
Qipao	旗袍	qípáo
Skirt	短裙	duǎnqún
Suit	西装	xīzhuāng
Underwear	内裤	nèikù

Others

Shoes	鞋子	xiézi
Boots	靴子	xuēzi
Cap/hat	帽子	màozi
Gloves	手套	shǒutào
Sandals	凉鞋	liángxié
Slippers	拖鞋	tuōxié
Socks	袜子	wàzi

Cosmetics

Cosmetics	彩妆	cǎizhuāng
Blush	腮红	sāihóng
Brow pencil	眉笔	méibǐ
Brow powder	眉粉	méifěn
Concealer	遮瑕膏	zhēxiá gāo
Eye liner	眼线	yǎnxiàn
Eye shadow	眼影	yǎnyǐng
Foundation	粉底	fěndǐ
Lipstick	唇膏	chúngāo
Loose powder	散粉	sǎnfěn
Makeup remover	卸装水	xièzhuāng shuǐ
Makeup removing lotion	卸装乳	xièzhuāng rǔ

深圳购物

Nail polish	指甲油	zhǐ jiǎ yóu
Nail polish remover	去甲油	qùjiǎyóu
Pressed powder	粉饼	fěnbǐng
Shimmering powder	闪粉	shǎnfěn

Electronics
Hardware

Backup Devices & Media	备份设备 & 媒体	bèifèn shèbèi&méitǐ
Barebones & Accessories	准系统及其配件	zhǔnxìtǒng& pèijiàn
CD / DVD Burners & Media	CD/DVD 刻录机&播放器	CD/DVD kèlùjī& bōfàngqì
Computer Accessories	电脑配件	diànnǎo pèijiàn
Computer Cases	电脑机箱	diànnǎo jīxiāng
CPUs / Processors	中央处理器/处理器	zhōngyāng chǔlǐqì
Fans & Heatsinks	风机&散热器	fēngjī& sànrèqì
Flash Memory & Readers	闪卡 &阅读器	shǎnkǎ&yuèdúqì
Hard Drives	硬盘驱动器	yìngpán qūdòngqì
Input Devices	输入设备	shūrù shèbèi
Memory	内存	nèicún
Monitors	显示屏	xiǎnshìpíng
Motherboards	主板	zhǔbǎn
Power Protection	电源保护	diànyuán bǎohù
Power Supplies	电源供应器	diànyuán gōngyìngqì
Printers & Scanners	打印机&扫描仪	dǎyìnjī& sǎomiáoyí
Projectors	投影机	tóuyǐngjī
Servers	服务器	fúwùqì
Sound Cards & MIDI Devices	声卡&MIDI设备	shēngkǎ & MIDI shèbèi
Speakers & Headphones	音箱& 耳机	yīnxiāng&ěrjī
Surveillance Cameras	监控摄像机	jiānkòng shèxiàngjī
Video Cards & Video Devices	视频卡&视频设备	shìpín kǎ &shìpín shèbèi

PC's

Desktop PCs	台式电脑	táishì diànnǎo
Laptops & Accessories	笔记本电脑&配件	bǐjìběn diànnǎo&pèijiàn
Laptops / Notebooks	手提电脑/笔记本电脑	shǒutí diànnǎo/ bǐjìběn diànnǎo

PDAs & Accessories

SHOPPING IN SHENZHEN

WWW.SZCITYGUIDE.COM

SHOPPING IN SHENZHEN

深圳购物

www.szCityGuide.com

PDAs & Accessories	掌上电脑&配件	zhǎngshàng diànnǎo&pèijiàn
Tablet PCs	平板电脑	píngbǎn diànnǎo
Ultra Mobile PCs	超便携式移动电脑	chāo biànxiéshì yídòng diànnǎo

Software

Business & Finance	商务&金融	shāngwù & jīnróng
Digital Media Editing	数码媒体编辑	shùmǎ méitǐ biānjí
Downloadable Software	下载软件	xiàzài ruǎnjiàn
Educational / Reference	教育/参考	jiàoyù/cānkǎo
Home Improvement & Hobbies	家居改造&爱好	jiājū gǎizào&àihào
Mac Games	Mac游戏	Mac yóuxì
Mac OS	Mac OS	Mac OS
Operating Systems	操作系统	cāozuò xìtǒng
PC Games	电脑游戏	diànnǎo yóuxì
Programming & Web Development	网页开发	wǎngyè kāifā
Security / Utilities Software	安全/实用软件	ānquán /shíyòng ruǎnjiàn
Server Software	服务器软件	fúwùqì ruǎnjiàn
Software Licenses	软件许可	ruǎnjiàn xǔkě

Networking

Firewalls	防火墙	fánghuǒqiáng
KVM Switches	KVM 交换机	kvm jiāohuànjī
Laptop Networking	笔记本电脑联网	bǐjìběn diànnǎo liánwǎng
Modems	网络调解器	wǎngluò tiáojiěqì
Networking Storage	网络存储	wǎngluò cúnchǔ
Servers	服务器	fúwùqì
Wired Networking	有线网络	yǒuxiàn wǎngluò
Wireless Networking	无线网络	wúxiàn wǎngluò

Games

Gamecube	GameCube 游戏机	GameCube yóuxì jī
Nintendo DS	任天堂 DS	rèntiāntáng DS
Nintendo Wii	任天堂Wii	rèntiāntáng Wii
PC Games & Accessories	电脑游戏&配件	diànnǎo yóuxì & pèijiàn
PS2	PS2游戏机	ps2 yóuxì jī
PS3	PS3游戏机	ps3 yóuxì jī
PSP	PSP游戏机	psp yóuxì jī

Video Game Console Accessories	视频游戏控制台配件	shìpín yóuxì kòngzhìtái pèijiàn
Video Game Consoles	视频游戏控制台	shìpín yóuxì kòngzhìtái
Xbox	Xbox 游戏机	Xbox yóuxì jī
Xbox 360	Xbox 360 游戏机	Xbox 360 yóuxì jī
Digital		
Camcorder Accessories	摄像机配件	shèxiàngjī pèijiàn
Camcorders	摄像机	shèxiàngjī
Digital Camera Accessories	数码相机配件	shùmǎ xiàngjī pèijiàn
Digital Cameras	数码相机	shùmǎ xiàngjī
Flash Memory	闪存	shǎncún
Mobile phones		
Bluetooth Headsets / Accessories	蓝牙耳机/配件	lányá ěrjī / pèijiàn
Mobile Phone Accessories	手机配件	shǒujī pèijiàn
Mobile Phone	手机	shǒujī
Hi-fi / Audio Video		
Audio Video Accessories	音频视频配件	yīnpín shìpín pèijiàn
Car Electronics	汽车电子产品	qìchē diànzǐ chǎnpǐn
Digital Photo Frames	数码相框	shùmǎ xiàngkuàng
Electronic Gadgets	电子小玩意	diànzǐ xiǎowányì
GPS & Accessories	全球定位系统&配件	quánqiú dìngwèi xìtǒng & pèijiàn
Headphones & Headsets	耳机&头带式耳机	ěrjī/tóudàishì ěrjī
Home Appliances	家电	jiādiàn
Home Audio	家用音响	jiāyòng yīnxiǎng
Home Video	家用视频	jiāyòng shìpín
Major Appliances	大家电	dàjiādiàn
Mobile Electronics	移动电子	yídòng diànzǐ
MP3 Players & Accessories	MP3 播放器&配件	mp3 bōfàngqì & pèijiàn
Office Equipment	办公设备	bàngōng shèbèi
Plasma / LCD / DLP TV	等离子/液晶显示器/ DLP电视	děnglízǐ/yèjīng xiǎnshìqì/DLP diànshì
Projectors	投影机	tóuyǐngjī
Telephones / VoIP	电话/网络电话	diànhuà/wǎngluò diànhuà

深圳购物

Tools, Hand & Power	工具，手动&电动	gōngjù, shǒudòng & diàndòng
Toys	玩具	wánjù
Apple		
Apple Accessories	苹果电脑配件	píngguǒ diànnǎo pèijiàn
Apple Desktops	苹果台式机	píngguǒ táishìjī
Apple Display	苹果显示屏	píngguǒ xiǎnshìpíng
Apple iPod Accessories	苹果iPod配件	píngguǒ iPod pèijiàn
Apple iPod Players	苹果iPod播放器	píngguǒ iPod bōfàngqì
Apple Laptops	苹果笔记本电脑	píngguǒ bǐjìběn diànnǎo
Mac Games	Mac游戏	Mac yóuxì
Mac Hard Drives	Mac硬盘	Mac yìngpán
Mac Memory	Mac记忆	Mac jìyì
Mac OS	Mac OS	Mas OS
Mac Software	Mac 软件	Mas ruǎnjiàn
Fabric		
Cashmere	羊毛	yángmáo
Cotton	棉	mián
Leather	皮	pí
Man-made textile	人造纺织	rénzào fǎngzhī
Natural fibre	天然纤维	tiānrán xiānwéi
Nylon	尼龙	nílóng
Silk	丝绸	sīchóu
Synthetic	人造的	rénzào de
Textile	纺织	fǎngzhī
Velvet	天鹅绒	tiān'é róng
Wool	羊毛	yángmáo
Flowers		
Lily	百合	bǎihé
Daisy	雏菊	chújú
Chrysanthemum	菊花	júhuā
Orchid	兰花	lánhuā
Rose	玫瑰	méiguī
Jasmine	茉莉	mòlì
Peony	牡丹	mǔdān
Narcissus	水仙花	shuǐxiān huā
Tulip	郁金香	yùjīnxiāng
Violet	紫罗兰	zǐluólán
Food & Drink		
Alcohols		

Beer	啤酒	pí jiǔ
Brandy	白兰地	bái lándì
Canned beer	罐装啤酒	guànzhuāng pí jiǔ
Champagne	香槟	xiāngbīn
Red wine	红葡萄酒	hóng pútáojiǔ
Rum	兰酒	lánjiǔ
Stout beer	黑啤酒	hēi pí jiǔ
Vodka	伏特加	fútèjiā
Whisky	威士忌	wēishì jì

At the market

Market	市场	shì chǎng
Amaranth (Chinese Spinach)	苋菜	xiàncài
Asian lettuce	生菜	shēngcài
Baby corn	小玉米	xiǎoyùmǐ
Bamboo shoots	竹笋	zhúsǔn
Bananas	香蕉	xiāngjiāo
Basil	罗勒	luólè
Black moss	发菜	fàcài
Bok choy	小白菜	xiǎobáicài
Broad beans	蚕豆	cándòu
Broccoli	西兰花	xī lán huā
carrot	胡萝卜	húluóbo
Cauliflower	花菜	huācài
Chayote	佛手瓜	fóshǒuguā
chestnut	栗子	lìzi
Chick peas	鹰嘴豆	yīngzuǐ dòu
Chinese cabbage	大白菜	dàbáicài
Chinese celery	芹菜	qíncài
Chinese kale (kalian)	芥兰	jièlán
Choy Sum	菜心	càixīn
Coriander or cilantro	香菜	xiāngcài
Corn	玉米	yùmǐ
Cucumber	黄瓜	huángguā
Eggplant	茄子	qiézi
Enokitake (golden mushrooms)	金针菇	jīnzhēngū
fruit	水果	shuǐ guǒ
Galangal	良姜	liángjiāng
Garlic	大蒜	dàsuàn
Ginger	姜	jiāng
Green soybeans	青豆	qīngdòu
hot pepper; chili; capsicum	辣椒	làjiāo
jicama	豆薯	dòushǔ

Kidney beans	菜豆	càidòu
Kohlrabi	球茎甘蓝	qiújīng gānlán
Lemongrass	柠檬 香茅	níngméng xiāngmáo
lotus root	莲藕	lián'ǒu
Mangoes	芒果	mángguǒ
Mung beans	绿豆	lǜdòu
Mung been sprouts	绿豆芽	lǜdòuyá
Onions	洋葱	yángcōng
Papayas	木瓜	mùguā
Peanuts	花生	huāshēng
Peas	豌豆	wāndòu
Plantains	芭蕉	bājiāo
Radish	萝卜	luóbo
Round cabbage	卷心菜	juǎnxīncài
Shallots	青葱	qīngcōng
Snow peas	糖荚豌豆	tángjiá wāndòu
Soy bean sprouts	黄豆芽	huángdòuyá
Soy beans	黄豆	huángdòu
Soy milk	豆乳	dòurǔ
Spinach	菠菜	bōcài
Sweet potatoes	地瓜	dìguā
Tempeh	印尼豆豉	yìnní dòuchǐ
Tofu	豆腐	dòufu
Vegetable	蔬菜	shūcài
Water chestnuts	荸荠	bíqi
Watercress	西洋菜	xīyángcài
Watermelon	西瓜	xīguā
Winter melon(white gourd)	冬瓜	dōngguā

Basic food

Basic food	食物	shíwù
Meat	肉	ròu
Beef	牛肉	niúròu
Chicken	鸡	jī
Duck	鸭	yā
Fish	鱼	yú
Pork	猪肉	zhūròu
Shrimp	虾	xiā
Butter	牛油	niúyóu
Cheese	芝士	zhīshì
Noodle	面	miàn
Snack	小吃	xiǎochī

Breads & Pastries

| Bread | 面包 | miànbāo |

深圳购物

SHOPPING IN SHENZHEN

www.szCityGuide.com

Cake	蛋糕	dàngāo
Cheese cake	芝士蛋糕	zhīshì dàngāo
Chocolate	巧克力蛋糕	qiǎokèlì dàngāo
Croissant	牛角面包	niújiǎo miànbāo
French baguette	法国棍子面包	fǎguó gùnzi miànbāo
Meat bun	肉包子	ròu bāozi
Pastry	糕点	gāodiǎn
Strawberry cake	草莓蛋糕	cǎoméi dàngāo
Tart	蛋塔	dàntǎ
Toast	土司	tǔsī

Fruits

Fruit	水果	shuǐguǒ
Apple	苹果	píngguǒ
Banana	香蕉	xiāngjiāo
Cherry	樱桃	yīngtáo
Coconut	椰子	yēzi
Durian	榴槤	liúlián
Grape	葡萄	pútáo
Kiwi	猕猴桃	míhóutáo
Lichee	荔枝	lìzhǐ
Mango	芒果	mángguǒ
Orange	橘子	júzi
Papaya	木瓜	mùguā
Peach	桃子	táozi
Pear	梨	lí
Pineapple	菠萝	bōluó
Strawberry	草莓	cǎoméi
Watermelon	西瓜	xīguā

Vegetable

Vegetable	青菜	qīngcài
Cabbage	卷心菜	juǎnxīncài
Carrot	萝卜	luóbo
Eggplant	茄子	qiézi
Mushroom	蘑菇	mógū
Pea	豌豆	wāndòu
Potato	土豆	tǔdòu
Pumpkin	南瓜	nánguā
Tomato	番茄	fānqié

Furniture

| Furniture | 家私 | jiāsī |

Bathroom

| Bathroom | 浴室 | yùshì |
| Bath lotion | 沐浴露 | mùyùlù |

Bathtub	浴缸	yùgāng
Carpet	地毯	dìtǎn
Chamber pot	马桶	mǎtǒng
Cleansing milk	洗面奶	xǐmiànnǎi
Mirror	镜子	jìngzi
Razor	剃刀	tìdāo
Rubbish bin	垃圾桶	lājī tǒng
Shampoo	洗发水	xǐfàshuǐ
Shaving scream	剃须膏	tìxū gāo
Toilet brush	马桶刷	mǎtǒng shuā
Toilet paper	卫生纸	wèishēngzhǐ
Toothbrush	牙刷	yáshuā
Toothpaste	牙膏	yágāo
Towel	毛巾	máojīn
Washing machine	洗衣机	xǐyī jī
Washing powder	洗衣粉	xǐyī fěn
Bedroom		
Bedroom	卧室	wòshì
Bed	床	chuáng
Desk	桌子	zhuōzi
Wardrobe	衣柜	yīguì
Carpet	地毯	dìtǎn
Chair	椅子	yǐzi
Crib	婴儿床	yīng'ér chuáng
Dressing table	梳妆台	shūzhuāng tái
Rubbish bin	垃圾桶	lājī tǒng
Ding room	食厅	shítīng
Napkin holder	餐巾纸架	cānjīnzhǐ jià
Carpet	地毯	dìtǎn
Chair	椅子	yǐzi
Dining table	餐桌	cānzhuō
Napkin	餐巾	cānjīn
Rubbish bin	垃圾桶	lājī tǒng
Toothpick	牙签	yáqiān
Cups & Glasses		
Cup	杯	bēi
Coffee cup	咖啡杯	kāfēi bēi
Glass	玻璃杯	bōli bēi
Tea cup	茶杯	chábēi
Wine glass	酒杯	jiǔbēi
Living room		
Living room	客厅	kètīng
Sofa	沙发	shāfā
Candle holder	烛台	zhútái

Chair	椅子	yǐzi
Coffee table	咖啡桌	kāfēi zhuō
DVD player	DVD机	DVD jī
Key rack	匙钥架	yàoshí jià
Rubbish bin	垃圾桶	lājī tǒng
Telephone	电话	diànhuà
TV	电视机	diànshì jī
Wall Vase	挂墙花器	guàqiáng huāqì

Kitchen

Kitchen	厨房	chúfáng
Cupboard	橱柜	chúguì
Carpet	地毯	dì tǎn
Detergent	洗洁精	xǐjié jīng
Rubbish bin	垃圾桶	lājī tǒng
Cooking utensils	厨具	chújù
Chopping board	砧板	zhēnbǎn
Egg-beater	打蛋器	dǎdàn qì
Microwave	微波炉	wēibō lú
Oven	烤炉	kǎolú
Pan	平底锅	píngdǐ guō

Material

Material	材料	cáiliào
Alloy	合金	héjīn
Crystal	水晶	shuǐ jīng
Ivory	象牙	xiàngyá

Outdoor Furniture

Outdoor Furniture	室外家具	shìwài jiājù
Beach chair	沙滩椅	shātān yǐ
Bench	长凳	chángdèng
Swing chair	秋千椅	qiūqiān yǐ
Material	材料	cáiliào
Cane	藤	téng
Red-lacquered	红漆	hóngqī
Wooden	木	mù

Study

Study	书房	shūfáng
Carpet	地毯	dì tǎn
Bookshelf	书架	shūjià
Business card holder	名片盒	míngpiàn hé
Chair	椅子	yǐzi
Computer	电脑	diànnǎo
Printer	打印机	dǎyìn jī
Rubbish bin	垃圾桶	lājī tǒng
Scanner	扫描仪	sǎomiáo yí

Tea

Tea pot	茶壶	cháhú
Tea set	茶具	chájù
Tea tray	茶盘	chápán
Caddy	茶罐	cháguàn
Utensils		
Chopsticks	筷子	kuàizi
Fork	叉	chā
Knife	刀	dāo
Plate	碟	dié
Spatula	铲	chǎn
Spoon	调羹	tiáogēng
Fruit plate	水果盘	shuǐguǒ pán
Coffee pot	咖啡壶	kāfēi hú
Plate rack	盘架	pánjià
Others		
Antique	古董	gǔdǒng
Modern	现代	xiàndài
Genuine	真品	zhēnpǐn
Imitation	仿造品	fǎngzào pǐn
Ornament	装饰品	zhuāngshì pǐn
Vase	花瓶	huāpíng
Jewelry		
Jewelry	首饰	shǒushì
Bracelet	手镯	shǒuzhuó
Earring	耳环	ěrhuán
Necklace	项链	xiàngliàn
Pendant	吊坠	diàozhuì
Ring	戒指	jièzhǐ
Brooch	胸针	xiōngzhēn
Stones		
Diamond	钻石	zuànshí
Ruby	红宝石	hóng bǎoshí
Pearl	珍珠	zhēnzhū
Jade	玉	yù
Crystal	水晶	shuǐ jīng
Material		
Material	材料	cáiliào
Gold plated	镀金	dùjīn
Silver	银	yín
Platinum	白金	báijīn
Gold	金	jīn
Bronze	铜	tóng
Shapes		
Shape	形状	xíngzhuàng
Teardrop	泪状	lèizhuàng

Leaf	叶状	yèzhuàng
Wing	翅状	chì zhuàng
Heart	心形	xīnxíng
Bead	珠状	zhūzhuàng

Kids

Toy	玩具	wánjù
Car	汽车	qìchē
Doll	洋娃娃	yángwáwá
Helicopter	直升飞机	zhíshēng fēijī
Plane	飞机	fēijī
Popgun	玩具枪	wánjù qiāng
Ship	船	chuán
Warship	军舰	jūnjiàn

Lights & Lamps

Lamp	灯	dēng
Bulb	灯泡	dēngpào
Lamp shade	灯罩	dēngzhào
Line light	吊线灯	diàoxiàn dēng
Pendant lamp	吊灯	diàodēng
Table lamp	台灯	táidēng
Wall lamp	壁灯	bìdēng
Wooden lamp	木灯	mùdēng

Pets

Pet	宠物	chǒngwù
Bird	鸟	niǎo
Cat	猫	māo
Dog	狗	gǒu
Fish	鱼	yú
Parrot	鹦鹉	yīngwǔ
Rabbit	兔子	tùzi
Turtle	乌龟	wūguī

Pharmacy

Aspirin	阿司匹林	āsīpǐlín
Bandage	绷带	bēngdài
Band-Aids	止血贴	zhǐxuètiē
Eye drop	眼药水	yǎnyàoshuǐ
Vitamin	维生素	wéishēngsù

Stationery

Stationery	文具	wénjù
Ballpoint (pen)	圆珠笔	yuánzhūbǐ
Compass	圆规	yuánguī
Eraser	橡皮	xiàngpí
Exercise book	练习本	liànxí běn
Fountain pen	钢笔	gāngbǐ

Gel pen	水笔	shuǐ bǐ
Globe	地球仪	dìqiú yí
Ink	墨水	mòshuǐ
Pencil	铅笔	qiānbǐ
Ruler	尺子	chǐzi
School bag	书包	shūbāo
Writing brush	毛笔	máobǐ
Color pencil	彩色铅笔	cǎisè qiānbǐ

Tailor

Belt	皮带	pídài
Button	钮扣	niǔkòu
Design	设计	shèjì
Dressmaker	裁缝师	cáiféngshī
High waistline	高腰	gāoyāo
Low waistline	低腰	dīyāo
Neckline	领口	lǐngkǒu
Normal waistline	中腰	zhōngyāo
Pocket	口袋	kǒudài
Sleeves	袖子	xiùzi
Waistline	腰围	yāowéi

Sizes

Size	尺寸	chǐcùn
Make it larger	弄大点	nòng dàdiǎn
Make it longer	弄长点	nòng chángdiǎn
Make it looser	弄松点	nòng sōngdiǎn
Make it smaller	弄小点	nòng xiǎodiǎn
Make it shorter	弄短点	nòng duǎndiǎn
Make it tighter	弄紧点	nòng jǐndiǎn
Size L	大码	dàmǎ
Size M	中码	zhōngmǎ
Size S	小码	xiǎomǎ
Size XL	加大	jiādà
Size XS	加小	jiāxiǎo
Size XXL	加加大	jiājiādà
Too large	太大	tài dà
Too long	太长	tài cháng
Too loose	太松	tài sōng
Too short	太短	tài duǎn
Too small	太小	tài xiǎo
Too tight	太紧	tài jǐn

Get your own Chinese Dictionary

WOULDN'T YOU LIKE to communicate in Chinese? Well, this is your chance. Get the best companion to learn, speak & write in Chinese...

我爱
汉语

EFFICIENCY

Professional English ⟷ Chinese dictionaries:

- ✓ Oxford Chinese English
- ✓ ABC Chinese English
- ✓ NWP Chinese English
- ✓ UNIHAN Database

STYLE

- ✓ Translate Chinese words by highlighting them directly on the screen

PERFORMANCE

- ✓ Learn to write Chinese characters by following the stokes

and much **more** ...

Visit now...

chinese.LonelyWriters.com

Shenzhen's Finest Cuisine

Chef Martin in Shenzhen   147

The Shenzhen Food Guide   152

Chef Martin in Shenzhen

THE WORLD-RENOWNED CHEF, Martin Yan, pioneered a daily TV Chinese cooking show, '*Yan Can Cook*' 30 years ago. With Chef Yan's warm, humorous and enthusiast characteristics, he quickly won a devoted group of fans. Chef Yan's entertaining show eventually developed into a culinary travelogue, featuring culinary hot spots throughout Asia.

Born in Guangzhou, China, Chef Yan possessed a passion for cooking at an early age. He formally began cooking at the tender age of thirteen as an apprentice at a popular Hong Kong restaurant. He later pursued an MS in Food Science at The University of California/Davis in the US. To put himself through university, Chef Yan gave Chinese cooking classes to his classmates and professors. His innate talent and flair for teaching was soon discovered and his career in the entertainment business skyrocketed.

Lets learn about Chef Yan's insight on Chinese cuisine and what he has been up to lately in Shenzhen.

CHEF MARTIN, WHAT ARE THE REGIONS OF CHINESE CUISINE?

CHINA'S CENTURIES OF culture and cuisine consists of various regions with their own distinctive flavors, techniques and ingredients. Over time, four classic regional cuisines developed – Mandarin 北京 in the north, Shanghai 上海 in the east, Cantonese 广东 in the south and Sichuan 四川 in the west.

The flavors in the north consist of a distinctive heavier seasoning, while in Shanghai sugar is commonly used. In the south, the chefs go easy on the seasoning and let the ingredients bring out their natural flavors. And Sichuan is known for its overwhelming spices and peppers, with beautiful colors.

CHEF MARTIN, WHAT REGION OF FOOD IS POPULAR IN SHENZHEN?

COMPARED WITH OTHER metropolitans, locals in Shenzhen do not prefer western food. This is probably because Shenzhen is a city of migrant workers from nearly all provinces; they still have not developed an understanding for western cuisine.

In the matter of Chinese cuisine, there is an abundance of varied regional Chinese cuisines in Shenzhen. The most popular one in Shenzhen is Cantonese, specifically the sub-regional, Chaozhou 潮州 cuisine. Many Chaozhou people have settled and started businesses here, so through the years they have become very successful. With their influence and wealth in the society, Chaozhou people have opened many restaurants for locals to enjoy. The cuisine is characterized by seafood as their staple and a mixture of light and fragrant tastes in the signature dishes.

CHEF MARTIN, WHAT IS GENERALLY THE PROMINENT CHINESE REGIONAL CUISINE KNOWN WORLDWIDE?

GENERALLY SPEAKING, WHEN people think of Chinese food, they are thinking of Cantonese style cuisine. Cantonese food is widely known outside of China because decades ago many southern Chinese people immigrated to other parts of the world to improve their life. When they settled in their new home they would open Chinese restaurants as their business and serve their home food. Because of this, people became more familiar with Cantonese food, but only know it as the broad term Chinese food. Today, more people are adventurous in trying other Chinese cuisine, so other regions like Sichuan 四川 flavors are becoming increasingly popular elsewhere.

CHEF MARTIN, HOW HAS CHINESE FOOD CHANGED OVER THE YEARS IN SHENZHEN?

WHEN CHEFS COOK their home food in Shenzhen, they must use local ingredients. Due to different climates, the ingredients' complexity is different from the native, which ultimately changes the flavor of the dish, bringing out other tastes it would not have originally. Also, with so many influences of different cuisines and chefs having some knowledge of all four regions, varied ingredients and techniques at times are fused together. It is still the traditional recipe but elements from another region are introduced to the original, creating a subtle flavor variation or alternative way of cooking. This is how the flavors and techniques of the Chinese cuisines have evolved in Shenzhen and many parts of China.

CHEF MARTIN, WHAT KIND OF CHINESE DELICACIES ARE THERE?

THERE ARE SO many – braised abalone, shark's fin soup, sea cucumber, swallow's nest and snake soup are all delicacies in China, but these are just a few.

CHEF MARTIN, WHAT PROJECTS ARE YOU INVOLVED IN SHENZHEN?

FOR QUITE A FEW years, my dream has been to establish a focal point to promote the Chinese culinary arts in response to the world's fascination of Chinese heritage and cuisine. So, I was searching for the perfect location all over China and finally found it in Shenzhen, next to Window of the World. Now, I have built my dream - Chef Martin Yan's Culinary Arts Center, (CAC) in Shenzhen. At CAC, we are a hub for oriental culinary exchange and a multi-level solution for corporate events. I developed this platform because I could not find a place for foreign chefs to learn about the beautiful history of China and the mystique of authentic oriental cuisine. When chefs go to France they can easily learn about French cuisine and tour the fresh produce markets. In Italy, it is the same. With CAC, I hope to give foreign chefs a chance to have hands on, intensive short-term exposure to the basics of Chinese cuisine. Programs for food enthusiasts are also offered, where they can watch exciting demonstrations or have hands on classes with various chefs at CAC's fusion restaurant – SensAsian.

CHEF MARTIN, why develop the Culinary Art Center (CAC)?

MANY PEOPLE IN other parts of the world see Chinese food only being served in a take-out-box, oily like sesame chicken – basically fast food. However, they have never had the chance to experience the authentic Chinese cuisine which is full of rich flavors, colorful ingredients and most of all, it is healthy. When an individual comes to CAC to learn about Chinese culinary arts and leaves having a different perspective of the cuisine, I am delighted. Each of these individuals shares with their family and friends that Chinese food is so much more, so that slowly, a greater number of people will appreciate it.

CHEF MARTIN, what is CAC's mission?

THERE ARE TWO angles to this question. Firstly, in the aspect of what we would like to achieve with Chinese food suited to the foreign taste: it is easy to create Chinese food. Anyone can cook Chinese food in their own household and it does not take much effort. My demonstrations are always an example of quick and easy preparations. The best part of Chinese food is generally very healthy. The seasoning added brings out the natural flavors of the ingredients, thus allowing us to absorb all the good nutrients. For example, to make a fish dish, all you need to add is some soy sauce, oil, slice of ginger and green onion, then pop it in to steam. Can you taste the tenderness of the meat melt into your mouth, while the seasonings accents the zest of the fish?

On the other hand, many local residents in Shenzhen do not know much about western dining. Through CAC's platform, we hope to provide locals with an experience of western etiquette, wine tasting and like workshops. Giving them this exposure will help them understand dining in a western atmosphere, and be more receptive to western food and culture.

CHEF MARTIN, WHY DID YOU CHOOSE SHENZHEN TO ESTABLISH CAC?

SHENZHEN IS SUCH a unique and fast growing metropolis it is hard not to choose this city. It's strategi-cally located in between Hong Kong, Guangzhou and Macau, which are all around one hour away. Then I also found this area in Overseas Chinese Town to house CAC that compliments my vision perfectly, with a beautiful European environment, South-East Asia's largest Ice-skating rink, easy accessibility to subway, and various grades of hotels. Going there is a true experience.

CHEF MARTIN, HOW DOES CAC COMPARE TO OTHER ESTABLISHMENTS IN SHENZHEN?

CAC IS VERY different from other individual and corporate establishments. The façade of the structure resembles a chateau and when you walk into our center or SensAsian restaurant, the feeling you perceive is very homely and warm. When individuals hold corporate team building training or private events at CAC, they are delighted by the quality services we provide. Plus, we accommodate to their needs and give then the unforgettable memory with colleagues, family and friends.

Pan-fried Snapper Fillet & Baby Lobster in Saffron Butter
煎脆香红鲷鱼柳及小龙虾配藏红花牛油 ▶

❶ Chef Martin's Culinary Art Center 甄文達大師廚藝中心

INTERESTED IN LEARNING more about the Culinary Art Center and joining culinary workshops, please contact the CAC at info@my-cic.biz or call +852 2858 7633 (Kong Kong office)

✉	Building 5, Oufeng Street, Window of the World, Nanshan (Next to Window of the World, City Inn) 南山区世界之窗欧风街5号楼 Post code: 518028 （在世界之窗的城市客棧）
✆	Tel: +86 755 2660 2923 Fax: +86 755 2660 2923
🚌	MTR: Window of the World Station -, Exit H1 世界之窗站，H1出口
⏳	SensAsian (Restaurant) opening hours: 11:30am – 10:30pm
🖱	www.mycac.biz info@mycic.biz

◀ **Glutinous rice wrapped with Strips of Beef** 牛肉糯米卷

Pan-seared scallops
干烧鲜带子 ▶

◀ **Teriyaki Chicken (with Dragon fruit)**
日式照烧鸡

The Shenzhen Food Guide

trip to Shenzhen, your worry should be not about whether you will find enough to eat; instead, you should be concerned about how to fit so many different kinds of food into a short visit.

I**N SHENZHEN, REST** assured you will not starve; you cannot starve. Even the most wary travellers are bound to find something comfortingly familiar, in the form of McDonald's, KFC, Pizza Hut, Starbucks and their ilk. That said, if you visit Shenzhen and eat every meal at U.S.-style fast food outlets, you will be missing out on the veritable treasure trove of culinary riches that the city has to offer. As a city populated largely by migrants from all over China, Shenzhen offers authentic food from almost every corner of the country; and with an ever-increasing expat population, southern China's boomtown also has a growing number of foreign food options. The city also has restaurants serving food tailored to different diets – vegetarians, despite the common perception that the Chinese diet consists of meat and more meat, have a great deal of choice, as do visitors who do not eat pork. Therefore, when planning your

Let's talk about the foreign food options first. With Japanese and Koreans making up the majority of expatriates in Shenzhen, it is no surprise that the city has a large number of restaurants serving these cuisines. Shenzhen has chains serving sushi and ramen, and also fine teppanyaki restaurants. As for Korean options, you'll be able to find the whole gamut of options, from barbecue to bulgogi. Southeast Asian choices include Thai (plentiful) and Malaysian (picking up). Similarly, if you're looking for European food, you will find French, German, Italian, Spanish and even Norwegian food here. South America is represented by the great number of Brazilian barbecue restaurants dotting the city. And Indian visitors feeling homesick have at least half a dozen restaurants to choose from.

■ Brought to you by Ranajit Dam, Shenzhen Daily www.szdaily.com - 深圳日报

深圳美食

SHENZHEN'S FINEST CUISINE

www.SZCityGuide.com

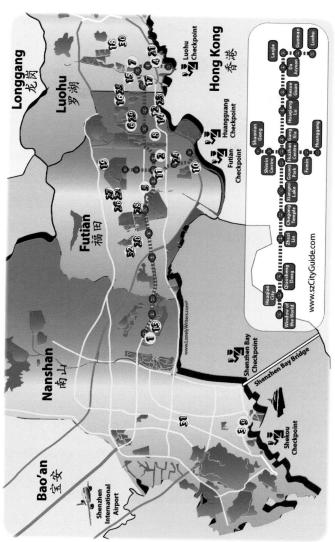

▲ **The Shenzhen Food Guide - 32 Restaurants**

Credits 林深

As MUCH OF a tourism advert as it is an eatery, Hanglipo is located on the first underground floor of Central Walk mall. However, despite the abundance of Malaysian flags and non-stop native Malaysian music, the restaurant warrants a trip because it's extremely good. Try the kangkung belacan (fried water spinach with spicy shrimp sauce), the ikan bakar (grilled fish with turmeric-based sauce) and the char kway teow (fried flat rice noodles.) While not prohibitively expensive, the place is not very cheap either, so it might be good idea to order set meals that are enough for two or three people.

➋ **Hanglipo Malaysian Fine Cuisine**	汉丽宝餐厅
✉	Hanglipo is located on the first underground floor of Central Walk mall. **Central Walk mall, Road Five, Fuhua Rd. 1 North,** Futian 福田区福华一路南中心五路怡景中心城
☏	+86 755 **8280 1399**
🚌	Bus: **3, 38, 50, 375** MTR: **Huizhan Zhongxin Station** - 会展中心站, **exit B**
⏳	**10am- 1am**

Credits 林深

WITH THE DEMISE of the Taco Bell Grande, the two Amigos eateries remain the last remnants of businesses' plans to introduce Tex-Mex food to the picky Shenzhen palate. Located in Shekou's Sea World area and Luohu, the Amigos restaurants are not strictly Tex-Mex, though; they have pastas and pizzas, English meat pies and even Japanese teppanyaki.

In the Mexican section of the menu, the chicken burrito with guacamole and sour cream has all three stated ingredients served liberally, but unfortunately no rice or refried beans. Also recommended are the beef tacos, served with a heap of cheese and the "classic" quesadillas with tomato salsa. Wash it all down with a jug of margarita.

❸ ❹ Amigos　　　欧蜜戈西餐厅

Outlet 1 - Nanshan 南山区

✉	1/F, Hong Long Hotel, Sea World, 32 Taizi Lu, Shekou, Nanshan 南山区蛇口32号太子路海上世界鸿隆公寓首层		
🚍	Bus: K105, K113, K204, 113,70, 226		
⏳	10am - 1:30am	☎	+86 755 2683 5449

Outlet 2 - Luohu 罗湖区

✉	Shop E6, G/F, Carriana Friendship Center, Renmin Nan Lu, Luohu 罗湖区罗湖人民南路佳宁娜广场1楼E06商铺		
🚍	Bus: 1,17,101 MTR: Guomao Station - 国贸站		
⏳	10am - midnight	☎	+86 755 6133 9993

Credits 承采

CRISPY BACON, THICK scrambled eggs and the sight of butter melting on piping-hot toast: sights to warm most hearts, but which, unfortunately are rarely seen in Shenzhen, the land of congee and fried dough. However, for expats and visitors who need a proper Western breakfast every morning, there's hope, or rather, there's Ihope.

It's all fairly cheap too, with full meals costing between two and three dollars US. So tuck into scrambled eggs, sausages and baked beans, and if you fancy something more lunch-like, Ihope offers sandwiches, salads, pizzas and hot dogs. Those with sweet tooth can choose between cheesecake and tiramisu. Free coffee refills most of the day.

⑤ **Ihope Cafe**	爱喝摩得咖啡
✉	Shop 106, 1F, Xin Hua Bao Xian Plaza, Mintian Lu, Futian (Next to Wall Street English) 福田区民田路新华保险大厦首层106铺(华尔街英语对面)
☎	+86 755 8826 4008
🚌	Bus: 373, 15
⏳	8am - 10pm

Credits 林深

FEW BUFFETS IN Shenzhen can even go close to matching Latin Grillhouse when it comes to value for money. Think five kinds of soup, salads, rice and noodle dishes, cold meat, cooked dishes, sushi, fruit and a wide range of desserts. And that, of course, was apart from the large portions of barbecued meat and vegetables that come by from time to time. And the options seemed endless; the permutations and combinations seemed mind-boggling. The chicken salami or the cold duck breast; the Japanese soybean fish or the curried chicken filet? Sushi or no sushi? Egg caramel, soufflé or rich chocolate fondue for dessert? Tough choices, these.

⑥ ⑦ Latin Grillhouse		拉丁餐厅
Outlet 1 - Futian 福田区		
✉	4F, Manha Shopping Plaza, Huaqiang Bei Lu, Futian 福田区华强北路曼哈购物广场四楼	
🚌	Bus: 75, 395	
⏳	8am - 10pm	☯ +86 755 **8322 2553**
Outlet 2 - Luohu 罗湖区		
✉	Floor 2,Xincheng Youyijie,No. 3085,Shennan Dong Lu,Luohu 罗湖区深南东路3085号新城又一街二楼	
🚌	Bus: 3, 12, 59, 103, 103B, 113 get off at Menzhen bu 门诊部 MTR: Laojie Station - 老街站, exit B	
⏳	08am - 10pm	
🖱	www.gzlatin.com	☯ +86 755 **8223 3665**

Credits 林珠

GIVEN HOW SHORT Shenzhen's own history is, Arirang Korean restaurant could claim to be a veritable city institution having been open in the busy Huaqiangbei area for more than a decade. Frequented by the city's Korean community – one sure guarantee of quality, authentic food - Arirang has an extensive menu, albeit slightly on the expensive side.

The stone pot rice is certainly recommended, lighter and more delicate than you'd expect. Also getting the thumbs-up is the goldongban, the Korean royal court version of bibimbap, comprising boiled rice mixed with steamed vegetables and roast beef. The restaurant also serves an array of soups, stewed and roasted mains and great oyster hotpot.

⑧ Arirang	阿里郎韩国料理
✉	Floor 2, Leizhen Building, No. 40, Fuming Lou, Futian 福田区福明路40号雷圳大厦2楼
✆	+86 755 8399 5099, 8399 5199
🚌	Bus: 301, 323, 216; get off at Shanghai Binguan 上海宾馆 MTR: Huaqiang Lu Station - 华强路站
⧗	10:30am - 11pm

Credits 林采

SHENZHEN'S FINEST CUISINE

www.szCityGuide.com

BOMBAY RESTAURANT ROSE from the ashes (debris, actually) of Little India which was destroyed by the Seaworld flood of the summer of 2007. The décor is similar, and like Little India, Bombay also serves neither beef nor pork to cater to both Hindu and Muslim diners. Go for the chicken pakora as a starter, along with the malai chicken tikka (55 yuan), a kind of chicken kebab marinated in creamy cashewnut sauce. For the mains, try the chicken butter masala, made with onion and tomato gravy, and the paneer kadai (40 yuan), with a capsicum base. An added bonus is the naan, which is as close to perfect as one can expect in Shenzhen, crisp and solid right to the end.

⑨ **Bombay Indian Cuisine & Bar**	印度餐
✉	**117,Sea World, Taizi Lu, Shekou,** Nanshan 南山区蛇口太子路海上世界117号
ℰ	+86 755 **2667 6049**
🚌	Bus: **70, 113, 204, K204, k113**
⏳	**Home delivery**

深圳美食

Credits 林深

THE NYPD IN NYPD Pizza stands for New York Pizza Delivery, but the owner's obviously trying hard to draw a connection with New York City Police Department. The delivery boys dressed in policemen's blue, and the restaurant logo similar to the officers' badge. No handcuffs just yet, but NYPD has begun to, er, "arrest" Shenzhen's palate with gigantic pizzas measures 16 inches in diameter, two more inches than the closest compe--titor in the city. NYPD Pizza prides itself on its pizza sauce, which is made from fresh tomatoes shipped from Modesto California, and is certainly worth dipping into with the crust, as is its barbecue sauce. The pizza crust is crisp and fluffy, and stays that way, right till the end. The toppings, comprising thick cheese with generous amounts of meat, include the staples: Hawaiian and Margarita, and also interesting ones like Curry Chicken.

⑩ ⑪ **NYPD Pizza**		纽约比萨
Outlet 1 - Futian 福田区		
✉	D1 Store, beside the underground parking entrance, Jun Huang Ming Ju, Futian 福田区福强路骏皇名居D1商铺(地下停车库入口旁)	
🚌	Bus: 4, 47, 52, 60 get off at Shuiwei cun 水围村. MTR: Fumin Station - 福民站	
⧗	9:30am - 10pm	☎ +86 755 8204 0503
Outlet 2 - Futian 福田区		
✉	FL-1015 Store, Central Walk, Fuhua 1Rd. Futian 福田区福华一路中心城 FL1015	
🚌	Bus: 3, 64. MTR: Huizhan Zhongxin Station - 会展中心站	
⧗	9:30am - 10pm	☎ +86 755 8887 6973

深圳美食

SHENZHEN'S FINEST CUISINE

www.SZCITYGUIDE.com

Credits 未来

9² DEGREES IS an iconic fixture on Shenzhen's dining scene. The original cafe, which opened in the first half of 2003, is near the Shangbu Building on Nanyuan Road at the border of Luohu and Futian districts. Atmospheric, dimly-lit and with an otherworldly ambience, the cafe's design harks back to some bygone era, with its timber floor, long, windows, hanging drapes old movie posters and so on. The new 92 Degrees Coffee Club in OCT has both indoor and outdoor seating and offers different kinds of soup, steak, fish dishes, spaghetti and dessert.

Try the cream of mushroom and spinach soup, the panfried codfish with garlic butter and the tiramisu for a satisfying meal in incredible surroundings. However numerous the foreign food options in Shenzhen are, they pale in comparison to the varieties of Chinese food available in the city. For Shenzhen is a city of migrants from all over China, most of whom have brought their food here with them. Here you can find northern dumplings and noodles, southern congee and dim sum, rough food from the far west and the sweetness and seafood of the coastal east

⑫ ⑬ **92 Degrees**		九十二度咖啡馆
Outlet 1 - Futian 福田区		
✉	72 Nanyuan Lu, Futian. 福田区南园路72号	
🚌	Bus: 14, 14B, 428. MTR: Kexue Guan Station - 科学馆站 - exit D	
⏳	9am - 3am	✆	+86 755 8362 9008
Outlet 1 - Nanshan 南山区		
✉	2/F, Huaxia Art Center, Nanshan. 南山区华夏艺术中心2楼	
🚌	Bus: 14,14B,63	
⏳	9am - 2am	✆	+86 755 2690 9139

深圳美食

Credits 林深

SERVING FOOD WITH maximum taste and minimum karma, Jinhaige, is the oldest Buddhist vegetarian restaurant in Shenzhen. It offers mock-meat, which approximates the aesthetic qualities of certain types of meat, a practice which goes back centuries. Try the succulent (mock) pineapple pork, and see if you can tell the difference between that and the real thing. The same goes for the black pepper beef, the fried mock chicken with mock mayonnaise, the mock shrimp balls and the spicy mock lamb skewers. The restaurant is popular among visiting Buddhist monks. A full list of items is available on Jinhaige's Web site www.szjhg.com.

⑭ ⑮ **Jinhaige**		金海阁
Outlet 1 - Futian 福田区		
✉	73, Nanyuan Lu, Futian. 福田区南园路73号	
🚌	MTR: Kexue Guan Station - 科学馆站 - exit D	
⏳ 9am - 10pm	☏	+86 755 8362 9008
Outlet 2 - Luohu 罗湖区		
✉	2F, Qinyuan Binguan, opposite Guiyuan Dianying Building, Luohu 罗湖区桂园路电影大厦对面（沁园宾馆2楼）	
⏳ 9am - 10pm	☏	+86 755 2556 3063
🖱	www.szjhg.com	

Credits 林深

BAGUALING FOOD STREET is one of those areas in Shenzhen that are open all night, with restaurants serving various kinds of food. Recommended among these is Xiaobaidu, which, offers Korean-style barbecued meat and vegetables. Part of a chain from Shenyang, the restaurant has comfortable four-seat booths which have individual grills to cook the meat on, complete with polythene aprons to prevent your clothes from getting sprayed with oil. Order the pork, the lamb, the sweet potato and the chicken gristle. Kimchee is also available on the side, and diners get complimentary lettuce (at least the first bowl anyway) to wrap the meat in. Down it all with some soju all the way from Korea.

⑯ **Xiaobaidu BBQ**	小百度烧烤店
✉	No.5, 1/F 10th Building Bagua Yi Lu, Futian 福田区八卦一路十栋首层5号
✆	+86 755 8242 9600
🚌	Bus: 352, 218
⏳	8am - 10pm

HAIFENG CUISINE HAS a great deal of seafood, which is often enhanced by piquant sauces, such as tangerine jam for steamed lobsters and broad-bean paste for fish. A good place to sample this is Jurenye Restaurant, which has outlets in Futian and Luohu districts. Try the stewed oysters with spring onion and ginger, a light yet flavourful dish which combines the pungent taste of spring onion with the spiciness of ginger. Also try the shrimp and pickle soup, which has a mildly sour broth, the omelette with shrimp and bitter melon, and the deep-fried pork with preserved tofu which is eaten wrapped in a lettuce leaf with a sweet-and-sour sauce

⑰ ⑱ ⑲ **Jurenye**	举人爷稻谷香

Outlet 1 - Luohu 罗湖区，宝安南店

✉	F1, Block3, No. 3033, Bao'an Nan Rd., Luohu 罗湖区宝安南路3033号3栋首层
☎	+86 755 2559 3444, 2589 3444
🚌	Bus: 18, 36, 225
⌛	11am - 10:30pm

Outlet 2 - Luohu 罗湖区，翠竹店

✉	F1, Cuibai Lou, Cuizhuyuan, cuizhu Road, Luohu 罗湖区翠竹路翠竹苑翠柏楼首层
☎	+86 755 2562 3444
🚌	Bus: 238, 23, 211 get off at Liuyi bu 留医部
⌛	11am - 3:30am

Outlet 3 - Futian 福田区，莲花店

✉	Floor3, Yiting Hotel, Lianhua Zhi Lu, Futian 福田区莲花支路逸庭宾馆三楼
☎	+86 755 6136 6928, 6136 6988
🚌	Bus: 219, 350; get off at Youxian Dianshi Tai 有线电视台
⌛	11am - 11pm
🖱	www.jurenye.com

Credits 林琛

Credits 唐报德

A CLASSY RESTAURANT SERVING Sichuan-Hunan fusion cuisine, Sanshisan Jiantang is most certainly worth a visit if you're a fan of spicy food. The place serves the best crab roe and tofu (蟹黄豆腐) in town, mixing the saltiness of crab roe with the thick, gooey tofu. Try the spicy shrimp (58 yuan), which features a big bucket of shrimp lounging languidly in a pond of oil, onion, garlic and peppers.

The fried boneless chicken with peppers (30 yuan) is yet another form of sensual assault, although less intimidating than the shrimp. Recommended, if you dare, is the bean jelly floating in oil. Make sure to a balance it all with a mild soup made of pulses.

❷⓿ **Sanshisan Jiantang**	三十三间堂
✉	Donghai Gouwu Guangchang, No.8099, Hongli Xi Lu, Futian 福田区红荔西路8099号东海购物广场
☎	+86 755 8837 1906
🚌	Bus: 228, 25, 10, 215, 236; get off at Huahui Shijie- 花卉世界
⏳	11am - 2pm, 5pm - 10pm

Credits 朵朵

ESTABLISHMENTS IN SHENZHEN that offer Xinjiang dishes are generally small and dingy, serving food in polystyrene bowls and with disposable chopsticks. In contrast, Zhongfayuan is large, spacious and well-lit. Order the lamb skewers, crispy outside and tender inside, slightly salty and hot. Also recommended are the fried sliced noodles (炒面片), cooked with bits of shredded lamb, the poached lamb (40 yuan), the four-vegetable treasure (boiled corn, snow peas, kidney beans and lily roots) and the dry-fried shrimp basket. The English translations in the menu are a bit wonky, though: What exactly is "insect grass dinner boiled dinner dark chicken?"

21 22 **Zhongfayuan**		中发源清真餐厅
Outlet 1 - Luohu 罗湖区，春风路店		
✉ No.2012, Chunfeng Rd., Luohu. 罗湖区春风路2012号		
☎ +86 755 8222 9318	⏳	10:30am - 0:30
🚌 Bus: 5,14,69 83 get off at Chunfeng Wanjia 春风万佳		
Outlet 2 - Futian 福田区，景田店		
✉ 1F, Wantuo Jiayuan, corner of Jingtian Rd. and Lianhua Rd., Futian. 福田区景田路与莲花路交汇处万托家园首层(妇儿大厦对面)		
☎ +86 755 8307 5126, 8307 5160	⏳	10am - 11pm
🚌 Bus: 6, 104, 328, 11; get off at Jingxin Huayuan 景新花园		
🖱 Many outlets in Shenzhen, check out www.zfxh.com		

Credits 朴涤

IF YOU'VE NEVER encountered the famous Shanxi roujiamou or "lamburger," Shanxi Hanji is a good place to try it. The roujiamo is griddle-steamed bread with lamb or pork filling. The meat is first boiled with wine, salt, rock candies, fresh ginger and shallot stems, and then more than twenty flavorings such as cardamom, clove, cinnamon and aniseed is added to it. After being cooked for 3 to 4 hours, the meat is then put into two pieces of freshly made griddle-steamed bread. The end-product resembles a sandwich, -- the steamed bread is tender and crisp, and the chopped meat is spicy and savory. Also try the zhajiangmian ("fried sauce noodles") comprising thick wheat noodles topped with a mixture of ground pork stir-fried with fermented soybean paste.

㉓ **Shanxi Hanji**	陕西韩记
✉	**158 Bading Street,** Futian 福田区巴丁街158号
✆	+86 755 **8236 6609**
🚌	Bus 14,62,63,214; **get off at** Bading Jie 巴丁街
⏳	**9am - 11pm**

Credits 补采

B RIGHT AND TASTEFULLY deco-rated Sichuan Douhua serves up a classic selection of Sichuan cuisine. The restaurant is well-known for its dozen varieties of jelly tofu, the most popular of which is the traditional style homemade jelly tofu, topped with crushed peanuts, spring onion, chili powder and soy sauce. Particularly recommended is the stewed fish with homemade chili sauce, which comprises Mandarin fish buried in red chili sauce. Also order the bangbang chicken and the dandan noodles, and finish the meal with sesame pie filled with taro mash (方芋夹). The restaurant provides complimentary soy milk, and a free bowl of longevity noodles to those celebrating their birthday.

24 25 26 Sichuan Douhua 四川豆花

Outlet 1 - Futian 福田区，彩田店

✉	Gangxia Shijie, Caitian Nan Lu, Futian. 福田区彩田南路岗厦食街		
✆	+86 755 8292 1479	⌛	9am - 4am
🚌	Bus: 113, 103, 212, 202 get off at Gangxia 岗厦. MTR: Gangxia St. - 岗厦站		

Outlet 2 - Futian 福田区，八挂一路店

✉	No. 11, Block 10, Bagua Yi Lu, Futian 福田区八卦一路十栋11号		
✆	+86 755 8226 4581	⌛	10am - 3:30am
🚌	Bus: 212, 352, 23		

Outlet 3 - Futian 福田区，景田店

✉	Floor 2,Jintai Shichang, Jingtian Bei Rd., Futian. 福田区景田北路金泰市场二楼		
✆	+86 755 8393 3629, 8393 3619	⌛	8am - 10pm
🚌	Bus: 11, 104, 6, 38, 73, 21; get off at Jingtian Bei 景田北		

Credits 林滨

SERVING A FUSION of Cantonese, Shanghai and Jiangxi cuisines, Meiluxuan (Idyllic Cottage) is a great place to eat prawns fried with tea leaves. Originally a Shanghai-style dish that comprises peeled prawns stir-fried with tea leaves; it is cooked in a different way at Meiluxuan. The unpeeled prawns are deep fried together with tea leaves, and to some extent resemble the signature Cantonese dish salty crispy prawns. While eating the prawns you will taste a slight hint of tea that is delicate and delightful. The crisp country-style chicken, a Cantonese-dish comprising farm-raised chicken finely roasted and served with a small tray of sweet-and-spicy sauce, is also worth a try.

㉗ **Meiluxuan**	美庐轩酒楼
✉	1,2/F, Zhenyejingzhou Building, Shangbao Road East, Futian 福田区商报东路振业景洲大厦一二层
☎	+86 755 8352 3411
🚌	Bus: 15, 25, 35, 73 Get off at Shangbao 商报站
⌛	9;30am -10pm

深圳美食

Credits 林深

MILLET GRUEL MAY not sound like the ideal hotpot broth, but it certainly has its advantages. The gruel retains the natural flavour of various ingredients, such as seafood and chicken cooked in it. Compared with the spicy and greasy Sichuan-style stock that removes the natural taste, the gruel is friendlier to the ingredients and retains more nutrition. A great place to try this is Xiangmixuan, which serves this type of hotpot along with a large variety of signature dishes from Shunde dishes, Guangdong province. Clams, chicken, fish balls and turnips are ingredients put into the broth. An array of sauces and seasonings, such as peanut, ginger, chili and onion sauces, and soybean oil and vinegar are available for diners. Interesting side dishes include pan-fried egg omelet with banana flower buds, and stewed alligator.

28 Xiangmixuan		香蜜轩酒楼
✉	Inside Xiangmihu Dujia Cun, Futian 福田区香蜜湖度假村内	
☎ +86 755 8331 1888	⏳	10am - 10pm
🚌 Bus: 21, 54, 59, 65 MTR: Xiangmihu Station - 香蜜湖站		

深圳美食

SHENZHEN'S FINEST CUISINE

www.szCityGuide.com

MR. M, A brand created by the well-known Sichuan restaurant chain Bashufeng 巴蜀凤, is discreet and classy. In addition to octagonal window frames, black wooden tables and chairs, Chinese calligraphy and artefacts, the waiters and waitresses are all dressed in long, dark robes, recreating the atmosphere of an ancient Chinese courtyard. The menu includes dishes from Sichuan, Guangdong and Shandong cuisines, and also has beef curry and gelato. Highly recommended is the braised pork, sweet and not greasy. Also try the poached peanuts decorated with rose petals, vegetables with fungi and deep-fried dumplings.

㉙ ㉚ ㉛ Mr. M 巴蜀凤

Outlet 1 - Futian 福田区，华强北店

✉	No.405, Sanda Xiaoqu, Zhenxin Lu, Futian 福田区振兴路桑达小区405号
☎	+86 755 8325 4969, 8324 6874
🚌	Bus: 375, 212
⏲	8:30am - midnight

Credits 林琛

Outlet 2 - Luohu 罗湖区，爱国路店

✉	Mutoulong Xiaoqu, No 34, Aiguo Lu. 罗湖区爱国路34号木头龙小区(近华丽路)
☎	+86 755 2568 0388
🚌	Bus: 104, 214
⏲	11am - 2pm, 5pm - 10pm

Outlet 3 - Nanshan 南山区，南山店

✉	Floor 2, Yuehai Zonghe Lou, No.104, Longcheng Lu, Nanshan 南山区龙城路104号粤海综合楼2楼
☎	+86 755 2649 2208
🚌	Bus: 329, 328, 217, 226, K113, 113, 437, 332, 433, 230, 204 Get off at Nanshan Youju 南山邮局
⏲	Weekdays: 11:30am - 2pm, 5:30pm - 10pm Weekends: 11:30am - 10pm

深圳美食

ANY TASTE FOR reptiles? Have fun in a very unusual restaurant where you'll find all sorts of reptiles and animals. Tortoises, snakes, fish and oysters, but also bee larvae… If you want to try any of these, no problem, you can chose them from the aquarium or the basket, chose your vegetable, your noodles or rice, and ask for a special recipe. Deep fried, boiled, steamed, sauté, chopped, in a soup or on a grill, all recipes are available, so bring a Chinese friend with you to help you and make sure you got the right taste. Savors and fragrances are delicious, all meals are different. Big tables outdoor with red lanterns and natural decoration, cosy seats in cane furniture. Have a go, you won't be disappointed.

■ This restaurant is brought to you by Isabelle Friedrich

㉜ **Yumizhixiang Restaurant**	渔米之香乡村酒家
✉	Nongke Center, Nongyuan Rd., Futian 福田区农园路农科中心
☎	+86 755 **8371 8821**, **8371 8831**
🚍	Bus: 105, 26, 326, get off at Nongke Zhongxin - 农科中心

深圳美食

SHENZHEN'S FINEST CUISINE

www.szCITYGUIDE.com

深圳美食

▲ Hotel Lobby The Intertlaken OCT © Hotel Shenzhen 深圳茵特拉根华侨城酒店

Luohu District 罗湖区

Crowne Plaza Hotel & Suites Landmark Shenzhen　深圳富苑酒店　178

Shangri-La Hotel Shenzhen　深圳香格里拉大酒店　179

Nanshan Districtt 南山区

Crowne Plaza Shenzhen　深圳威尼斯皇冠假日酒店　180

Cruise Inn Hotel Shenzhen　深圳鸿隆明华轮酒店　181

Fraser Place Shekou　深圳泰格公寓　182

Inter-Continental Shenzhen　深圳华侨城洲际大酒店　183

Kempinski Hotel Shenzhen　深圳凯宾斯基酒店　185

Nanhai Hotel　深圳南海酒店　187

Futian District 福田区

Four Points by Sheraton Shenzhen　深圳福朋喜来登酒店　188

Marco Polo Shenzhen　马哥孛罗好日子酒店　189

Sheraton Shenzhen Futian　深圳福田喜来登酒店　190

Bao'an District 宝安区

Mission Hills Resort　深圳骏豪酒店　191

Yantian District 盐田区

The Intertlaken OCT Hotel Shenzhen　深圳茵特拉根华侨城酒店　192

Sheraton Dameisha Resort　深圳大梅沙京基喜来登度假酒店　194

GETTING A GOOD night's sleep is a lot easier in Shenzhen than it used to be. There are many new hotels that have opened in the last couple years with more on the way. Now it's just a matter of choosing the location that works best for you.

Originally all the major businesses and shopping took place in the Luohu district 罗湖区 near the major train station. This area is still a top choice for shopping with Dongmen, King Glory Mall and of course the Luohu Commercial City (Mecca for all things). If you are visiting Shenzhen for business, Futian district 福田区 has many new international standard hotels. This is the place to be if you are attending a trade fair at the Shenzhen International Convention Center or need to be near the government offices. Got the kids in tow? Shenzhen has plenty of theme parks to keep them happy. The Overseas Chinese Town 华侨城 area in Nanshan district 南山区 is the place for you. Nanshan's Shekou 南山区蛇口 area

is Shenzhen's unofficial expat ghetto. This is where you will want to stay for fun, restaurants and Western oriented culture. The ferry to Hong Kong and Hong Kong Airport is in this neighborhood as well.

What if you just need a beach break or really want to get away from the city? Check out the resorts in the Eastern area of Yantian District 盐田区 or head to the hills in Bao'an District 宝安区 for an incredible golf and spa experience. You can contact the hotels directly or check out www.ctrip.com, www.elong.com, or www.sinohotels.com to compare prices.

Like everything else in China if you are dealing directly with the hotel ask about promotional or special rates. Make sure you bring along a copy of the hotel's name and address in Chinese as Shenzhen taxi drivers are not usually English speaking.

■ Brought to you by
Mary Ann MacCartney

Rates are based on comparing the hotels own websites and popular search engines like elong.com and orbitz.com and asiahotels.com for Friday June 20th 2008.

$$$$	RMB 1301+
$$$	RMB 1101 - 1300
$$	RMB 801 - 1100
$	RMB less than 800

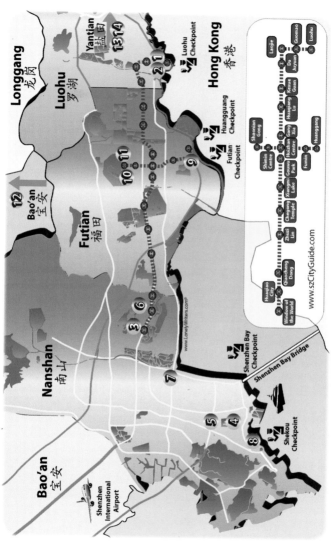

▲ Shenzhen's Best Hotels

① Crowne Plaza Hotel & Suites Landmark Shenzhen 深圳富苑酒店

THE CROWNE PLAZA Landmark Hotel is a very comfortable traditional hotel designed with the business traveler in mind. Guest rooms are nicely decorated in a conservative style with high quality fittings. The color scheme is gold and navy with dark wood floors and mahogany furniture. As the hotel is in the middle of a very busy commercial area the windows are thoughtfully double glazed. There is a wide range of room types. There are a few standard rooms which are the smallest at 36 m² (Net 28 m²) and do not have a tub. TVs in these rooms are 26" LCD. Most rooms are much larger at 48 m² or 64 m² with 42" LCD TVs. All rooms have broadband internet, laptop size safes, voice mail, and separate make up area, robes, steam irons and lovely bathrooms with rainforest showers. The Studio rooms are 64 m² with extra large beds (2.1m x 2.2m), free broadband internet, extra deep two person bathtubs, fax machines and DVD players. These rooms and the suites have private butler service which can handle packing, travel arrangements, translations, laundry and valet service. The butlers have been trained by the English Guild of Professional Butlers. The hotel's club level offers the usual amenities of a cooked buffet breakfast, lunch and dinner snacks, cocktails and hors d'oeuvres, separate check-in and butler service. The smallest rooms are a bit cramped and considering the difference in price is minimal, this is one hotel where getting a room upgrade is a good investment. ♔♔♔♔♔

✉	**3018 Nanhu Road,** Luohu 罗湖区南湖路3018号	

	Phone	+86 755 8217 2288
☏	**Fax**	+86 755 8229 0479
	Web	www.crowneplaza.com
	Email	crowneplaza-landmark.sz@ihg.com

Total Number of Rooms	230	**Std. Room Rate**	$

深圳顶级酒店

SHENZHEN'S BEST HOTELS

WWW.SZCITYGUIDE.com

② Shangri-La Hotel Shenzhen 深圳香格里拉大酒店

THE SHANGRI-LA HOTEL Shenzhen is located in the Luohu district adjacent to the busy Hong Kong border, the train station and the major shopping center for bargain hunters, Luohu Commercial City. As Shenzhen's original (built in 1992) five star hotels it has held up fairly well but it is by no means the best address in town nowadays. Guest rooms are typical of their era at 30 m². The decorations in the newly renovated rooms are in taupe and brown and contemporary. Non-renovated rooms are sad with dated décor, stained carpets and a stale smell. The beds are Chinese style firmness (hard). All rooms have free of charge broadband Internet TVs are standard boxes. There is coffee/tea making facilities, mini bar, and safe, IDD telephones with voice mail and central AC with individual controls. The bathrooms are a bit dated but passable. Robes and slippers are standard. Avoid rooms on the lower floors and those that have not been renovated. Noise is an issue because of the hotel's location. Do check out the 360° Bar & Restaurant on top of the hotel. The view and the décor are outstanding. The Shangri-La Shenzhen is overall a good property with a convenient location for those who are transiting either Hong Kong or Guangzhou via rail or are ready to do some serious shopping.

✉ East Side, Railway Station, 1002 Jianshe Road, Luohu
罗湖区建设路火车站东侧

Phone	+86 755 8233 0888
Fax	+86 755 8233 9878
Web	www.shangri-la.com
Email	slz@shangri-la.com

Total Number of Rooms	553
Std. Room Rate	$ $

③ Crowne Plaza Shenzhen 深圳威尼斯皇冠假日酒店

THE 17-STOREY CROWNE Plaza Shenzhen is a theme hotel, one of three owned by the Overseas Chinese Town group. In this case the theme is Venice and the hotel's name in Chinese means Venetian. Bell staff wears gondolier costumes and the décor is supposed to look like Italy, but this is a considerable stretch of the imagination. The hotel has indoor and outdoor swimming pools, a very large fitness center with certified personal trainers, sauna and steam facilities. The spa specializes in Hydrotherapy treatments. Other amenities include a beauty shop, gift shop and a self service laundry. A small shopping arcade features some nice gift items as well as sundries The hotel is surrounded by theme parks which include Window of the World (all the world monuments replicated in miniature), Splendid China and the Chinese Cultural Villages (see all of China in an day) and Happy Valley an amusement park. This makes this hotel a great choice for families or those with limited time in China. Guest rooms range from 32 m² to 50 m² and are neutral albeit uninspiring in the plain beige décor with about 60% featuring balconies. The beds are typical Chinese (very firm). The Crown Plaza Shenzhen is a good hotel that manages to satisfy the needs of both the business and leisure traveler. The staff is pleasant and efficient even if they do look funny in their costumes. ♦♦♦♦

	No. 9026 Shennan Ave., Overseas Chinese Town (OCT), Nanshan 南山区华侨城深南大道9026号
Phone	+86 755 2693 6888
Fax	+86 755 2693 6999
Web	www.crowneplaza.com
Email	cpsz@cpsz.com
Total Number of Rooms	372
Std. Room Rate	$$

④ Cruise Inn Hotel Shenzhen 深圳鸿隆明华轮酒店

IF YOU ALWAYS wanted to take a cruise but were afraid you might get seasick this is the hotel for you. Previously a French cruise ship, this unique hotel is now land-locked in the heart of Shekou's festive Seaworld Plaza. The guest rooms are surprisingly large (each is made up of two former state-rooms). The decoration is nautical, surprise! Inside the hotel there is a big German Restaurant and a sports bar as well as a Brazilian Barbecue Restaurant, but with so many options in the plaza below you may choose other less expensive options. If noise or privacy is a concern, request a room overlooking the golf driving range and not the plaza. This is a fun property.

✉	Minghua Ship Sea World Plaza Taizi Road, Shekou, Nanshan 南山区、蛇口 太子路海上世界广场明华轮	
☎	Phone	+86 755 2682 5555
	Fax	+86 755 2689 2666
	Web	www.honlux.com
	Email	reservations@honlux.com
Total Number of Rooms		110
Std. Room Rate		$

Credits SKQQa

Shenzhen's Best Hotels

www.szCityGuide.com

深圳顶级酒店

⑤ Fraser Place Shekou 深圳泰格公寓

FRASER PLACE SHEKOU, Shenzhen is nestled on the hillside in one of Shekou's upscale residential neighborhoods. Built in 2006, its sleek attractive profile is modern and attractive. Within walking distance of the hotel are the major banking and office buildings of Shekou as well as the entertainment district of Seaworld. The ferry terminal is a five minute drive while Shenzhen Airport is 25 minutes away. Accommodations are geared towards the long term guest with kitchens, combination washer and dryers, satellite television, CD and DVD players, high-speed Internet connections, multi-line phones, safes and complimentary toiletries. The décor is contemporary and attractive. The smallest units are one bedroom studios (35 m²) which are a basic hotel room. The one-bedroom deluxe are a generous 75 m² while the one-bedroom premier is 113 m². Two bedroom units range from 147 m² -171 m², Three-bedroom units range from 198 m² to 286 m² while the penthouse four bedroom units are either 248 m² or 419 m². Larger units all have a full kitchen with multifunctional microwave oven, hob and hood, refrigerator, toaster, electric kettle, fine bone china, glassware, rice cooker, cutlery and crockery. The beds are unfortunately rock hard. The bathrooms are modern with separate shower and tubs. For multi bedroom apartments there is a bathroom for each bedroom. Most rooms have balconies. If you are going to be in Shenzhen for a long visit this is definitely the best option in the area.

| ✉ | **8 Nanhai Road (former Industrial Road),** Shekou, Nanshan |
| | 南山区、蛇口南海大道8号 |

☏	Phone	+86 755 2688 3333
	Fax	+86 755 2688 5706
	Web	shekou.frasershospitality.com
	Email	sales.shenzhenshekou@frasershospitality.com

| **Total Number of Rooms** | 232 | **Std. Room Rate** | $$ |

⑥ Inter-Continental Shenzhen 深圳华侨城洲际大酒店

OPENED IN 2007, the Inter-Continental Shenzhen is, for the moment, the most glamorous and luxurious hotel in the city. The location on Shennan Road is midway between the Downtown and the airport (25 minutes drive). It is walking distance to Splendid China and the Chinese Cultural Folk Villages which are major Chinese theme parks. Like its sister properties the Crown Plaza Shenzhen and the Interlaken OCT Hotel, this property is owned by the Chinese Overseas Town group. It also sports a theme; this time all about Spain. The obsequious Chinese staff greet guests in electric orange matador jackets with shocking pink tights (the men) or red, black and white polka dot flamenco dresses (the ladies). In a case of too much of a good thing, these well-meaning young staff swamps guests with attention. The huge lobby is a dramatic work of art combining traditional Spanish architecture with a domed ceiling and avant-garde decorations in black, white and red with occasional splashes of orange. It gets your attention. The guest rooms are spacious (min 50 m²) and very well appointed. The décor is Spanish contemporary with blonde wood and soft tones complemented by earthy red accents. Windows are double-glazed and the views are either of the pool or looking out on the hills of Hong Kong's New Territories. Most rooms have balconies. All rooms have complementary newspaper, turndown service, cable 37" LCD TVs, DVD/CD players, Bose stereo sound system, coffee and tea maker, mini bar and a good work desk. Internet access is free both wired and wireless. The bathrooms are fabulous and chic with a dedicated vanity bar, 15" LCD TVs and rain forest shower with separate oversized bath. The Inter-Continental Shenzhen is an excellent hotel with a great décor with a quirky sense of humor. It is easily the most luxurious hotel in the city (at least until the new Ritz Carlton and Shangri-La's open in 2008). The hotel's major flaw is the inexperienced staff. For the prices charged in the food and beverage outlets, this is a disappointment. ♦♦♦♦♦

⑥ Inter-Continental Shenzhen 深圳华侨城洲际大酒店

✉	9009 Shennan Ave., Nanshan 南山区华侨城深南大道9009号

☎	Phone	+86 755 3399 3388
	Fax	+86 755 3399 3399
	Web	www.ichotelsgroup.com
	Email	reservations@icshenzhen.com

Total Number of Rooms	549
Std. Room Rate	$ $ $

Nanshan Shekou - Credits 韦洪兴

深圳凯宾斯基酒店

SHENZHEN'S BEST HOTELS

WWW.SZCITYGUIDE.COM

深圳顶级酒店

⑦ Kempinski Hotel Shenzhen 深圳凯宾斯基酒店

OPENED IN 2006, the Kempinski Hotel Shenzhen is a deluxe property located in Shenzhen's Nanshan District. When it first opened it was surrounded by construction sites and was not a particularly pleasant area, but this is China and things change quickly. Now there is a large upscale shopping mall, an in-door ice skating rink, Poly Theatre, a 1700 seat futuristic auditorium and lots of upscale residential high rises. Shenzhen Bay Bridge which links the city to Hong Kong is a five minute drive and a subway line will be opening in 2010. The hotel's exterior is high-rise and not especially note worthy so one is taken aback by the breathtaking circular lobby with a massive glass gold and red object d'art cum chandelier hanging from the ceiling. It resembles a giant stylized torch. This motif is repeated throughout the golden lobby. Mosaic black and gold floors add drama to an already theatrical space. The smallest of the contemporary guest rooms, Superior, are 32 m² while the Deluxe rooms are a bit more spacious at 35 m². What they lack in size is made up for in amenities.

All rooms have free high speed broadband Internet access, IDD/DDD telephone with voicemail. Phone calls within China are free of charge. 32" LCD TVs are standard with 43 satellite international TV & Radio channels. Electrical outlets are dual voltage (110V/220V). Most of the rooms feature Super King beds with Western pillow top mattresses. The rooms have safes, mini bar, coffee and tea making facilities, bottled drinking water, and fresh fruit, turn down service, bathrobes and slippers. Bathrooms are sleek and modern with the usual hairdryer and bath amenities including an adjustable shaving/make up mirror, separate rain forest shower and bath tub. There are 20 dedicated Ladies Executive rooms with special amenities such a pink robes and flowered sheets. The Kempinski's glamorous look has won it a lot of fans but the rooms are disappointingly small for a new deluxe hotel. For those doing business in Shenzhen's Hi-Tech Zone or needing easy access to Hong Kong the location is good but it is still a neighborhood in the process of finding itself. ♦♦♦♦♦

⑦ Kempinski Hotel Shenzhen 深圳凯宾斯基酒店

✉	Hai De San Dao, Houhaibin Road, Nanshan 南山区后海滨路海德三道

✆	Phone	+86 755 8888 8888
	Fax	+86 755 8612 3999
	Web	www.kempinski-shenzhen.com
	Email	reservations.shenzhen@kempinski.com

Total Number of Rooms	390
Std. Room Rate	$ $

Window of the World - Credits 韦洪兴

⑧ Nanhai Hotel 深圳南海酒店

BUILT IN 1986, the Nanhai Hotel is located in Shenzhen's Shekou area, adjacent to the ferry terminal for Hong Kong city and airport as well as Macau and Zhuhai ferries. Once one of the best hotels in the city the Nanhai is now past her prime and in need of a face lift. Guest rooms are a mixed bag. The lowest room category and the apartments are in need of a drastic face lift. Mint green lavatories and sinks scream the 1980s. The newly renovated rooms are on the other hand quite attractive with wooden floors and balconies (oddly without furniture). The decorations are contemporary Asian with dark wood and comfortable seating areas. Rooms are around 28 m² and the bathtub and shower are combined but they are attractive with nice amenities. Robes and slippers are standard as are hair dryers, mini bar, electronic safe and broadband internet access. TVs with satellite stations are standard 25" box style. Beds are extremely hard. The Nanhai's location next to the ferry terminal is its best asset. The high speed ferry can whisk visitors to Hong Kong International Airport in 30 minutes or downtown Hong Kong in 50 minutes. Unfortunately the hotel has not kept up with the times and needs a lot of work to bring into line with the newer hotels cropping up. ⬦⬦⬦

✉	1, Gongye 1st Road, Shekou, Nanshan 南山区、蛇口工业区工业一路1号	
ℂ	Phone	+86 755 2669 2888
	Fax	+86 755 2669 2440
	Web	www.nanhai-hotel.com
	Email	nh@sz-nanhaihotel.com
Total Number of Rooms		396
Std. Room Rate		$

⑨ Four Points by Sheraton Shenzhen 深圳福朋喜来登酒店

THE FOUR POINTS by Sheraton Hotel is located near to the Huanggang border into Hong Kong in Shenzhen's Futian District. Surrounding the hotel are hi-tech and logistic companies. The large lobby is contemporary and attractive. The hotel has made a name for itself with its high quality dining options which is a good thing as there is no other retail or dining options nearby. It is geared towards business travelers with very good meeting facilities. Other amenities include a spa, indoor pool and nice fitness center. Rooms are pretty standard at 30 m². All have good quality Western style mattresses and free hi-speed internet. The decoration is pleasant and bathrooms feature rain forest showers. If your business brings you to this part of Shenzhen the Four Points is a reliable albeit bland choice. ♦♦♦♦♦

✉	Free Trade Zone, No. 5 Guihua Road, Futian 福田区桂花路5号, 福田保税区	
☏	Phone / Fax Web Email	+86 755 8359 9999 / +86 755 8359 2988 www.fourpoints.com/shenzhen reservations.shenzhen@fourpoints.com
Total Number of Rooms	278	Std. Room Rate	$

Check out the 6th floor ! Opening in August '08...

Divine Lounge: A place to perch & pose; feminine design with unique curved entrance feature.

The terrace: Panoraminc views of the river and hills of Hong Kong beyond roof top landscaped gardens.

Club room: The DJ is the king in this club. Set on a pedestal and thrust into the center of the room, the DJ is surrounded by the clubbers. VIP deck on raised floor with excellent sight lines.

Tapas Cafe Bar: Taste the Mediterranean cafe style continental dining. Theatrical open kitchen feature.

Bullion Bar: Open all day. The Bullion Bar is a place to meet, great and have discrete business meetings away from the hustle and bustle of everyday office environment

⑩ Marco Polo Shenzhen

马哥孛罗好日子酒店

THE MARCO POLO Shenzhen opened in 2006. It is a modern tower building located in the business and government Futian District in downtown Shenzhen. It is conveniently located near to the Shenzhen International Convention and Exhibition Centre and the Subway and 25 minutes to both the Shekou Ferry Terminal and Shenzhen Bao'an Airport. The spacious contemporary atrium lobby has a dramatic staircase that leads to the meeting facilities on the next level. The ambiance is business like with doormen and registration staff being efficient and English speaking. The guest rooms are on levels 19 – 34 (an office building is below). All rooms have a clean, fresh contemporary décor with blonde wood, dark blue, soft gray and white accents.

Rooms have large windows with a great view of the downtown. Amenities include free of charge broadband Internet access, LCD TV monitors, electronic safe, separate shower and bath, coffee / tea making machine, electronic door lock, air conditioning, business-sized desk with multifunction adapters, alarm clock, and two-line speakerphone. The lowest room category, Superior, is 30-32 m². Deluxe rooms are roomier at 35 m² while deluxe premier are 40 m². The hotel caters primarily to the domestic market so the beds are of an Asian firmness (ouch!) Corner rooms are coveted because of the windows on both sides. The Marco Polo Shenzhen is a good hotel with better than average meeting space and an excellent location for the business traveler.

✉	Fuhua 1st Road, Futian 福田区福华一路	
☎	Phone	+86 755 8298 9888
	Fax	+86 755 8298 9888
	Web	shenzhen.marcopolohotels.com
	Email	Shenzhen@marcopolohotels.com
Total Number of Rooms	391	Std. Room Rate	$$

⑪ Sheraton Shenzhen Futian

深圳福田喜来登酒店

THE SHERATON SHENZHEN Futian is a gleaming black art deco skyscraper that opened in 2006. It is located in the heart of Shenzhen's new central business district between the Shenzhen Convention & Exhibition Center and Shenzhen Civic Center, and directly accessible to Shenzhen's Metro. The cavernous, garish and masculine lobby is done in gold, black and lots of marble. A large crystal chandeliers accent the high ceiling. The hotel is owned by a Chinese company whose corporate symbol is a falcon. In seeming homage to Dashiell Hammett, enormous gold falcon statues are the dominate decoration in the lobby and in the meeting spaces. The masculine feel continues in the guest rooms which are spacious and well appointed in brown and gold shades and dark wood. They all feature the Sheraton Sweet Sleeper bed (Ahh…). Bathrooms are large with a separate rainforest shower and tub. 32" plasma TVs are standard with satellite channels. Mini bar, iron/ironing board, robes, dual line telephone, in room safe and a free daily newspaper is standard. Wireless internet as well as broad band is available at an additional charge. The hotel's website and brochures are deceptive as many of the features advertised are not yet completed. Currently the hotel competes with the Marco Polo Shenzhen. In 2008 when the new Ritz Carlton and Shangri-La Futian open nearby this property will have some serious competition. For now the central location, meeting facilities and the comfortable rooms are the strongest selling points. ◆◆◆◆◆

✉	Great China International Exchange Square, Fuhua Road, Futian 福田区福华路大中华国际交易广场		
☎	Phone	+86 755 **8383 8888**	
	Fax	+86 755 **8383 8998**	
	Web	**www.starwood.com**	
	Email	Shenzhen.sheraton@sheraton.com	
Total Number of Rooms	280	**Std. Room Rate**	$$

(12) Mission Hills Resort

深圳骏豪酒店

STRETCHING ACROSS SHENZHEN and Dongguan, Mission Hills is the World's No.1 golf club with a whopping 216 holes and 12 courses designed by 12 world-renowned golf legends. Aside from golf the resort also features 6 driving ranges, a huge golf shop, 51 tennis courts, a recreation center with library, billiards, table tennis, archery, gym, library, sauna and steam baths, massage, acupuncture, cycling and Chinese medical massage. The resorts spa has 10 couple and 5 single treatment suites with private bathtub, shower and dressing rooms. Highlights include hydrotherapy treatment rooms with hydro massage bathtubs, dry flotation beds and Vichy showers, a yoga pavilion and an outdoor qu gong deck. Guest rooms in the hotel wing all have a great view of the golf course. The smallest room category, deluxe, is a generous 45 m²; grand deluxe rooms are 55 m² with balconies. Premier suites are 100 m² with separate living and bedroom areas and a large greeting area suitable for yoga and Taichi session. The bathrooms have a Jacuzzi tub facing the golf course. The décor is a nothing terribly special, but with all the recreation options you are unlikely to spend much time in the room. ♦♦♦♦

✉	1 Mission Hills Road, Bao'an 宝安区骏豪1号	
☎	Phone Fax Web Email	+86 755 2802 0888 +86 755 2801 1111 www.missionhillsgroup.com reservation@missionhillsgroup.com
	Total Number of Rooms	315
	Std. Room Rate	$$

⑬ The Interlaken OCT Hotel Shenzhen 深圳茵特拉根华侨城酒店

ADD TO THE list of '*only in China*'. A luxury alpine resort hotel replicating a Swiss village with Chinese folks dressed in lederhosen sitting in subtropical southern China. The Interlaken OCT (Overseas Chinese Town) Hotel is set in the hills of Eastern Shenzhen. It is part of an enormous theme park development that includes the hotel, 10,000 m² spa, antique train, Eco Park and Theatre. Opened in 2007 the hotel caters primarily to the domestic market who presumably has never been to Europe much less a real alpine village. The location is about an hour from Shenzhen airport and 30 minutes from downtown Shenzhen. As part of a 9 square kilometer theme park there are plenty of unique recreational outlets including the Wind Valley Golf Club, the Interlaken Spa, China's largest indoor and outdoor mineral spring spa, Sanzhou Tea Garden and a unique Tea Show which features a Zen theme with sound and light.

The Cuckoo Clock stage has an outdoor performance hourly during the day. Nearby tennis courts are available as well as three themed villages replete with gingerbread facades. Inside the hotel there is a fitness center. Guest rooms are spacious at 56 m². The decoration is opulent with a distinctly European panache. Rooms have 42-inch LCD TVs, large modern writing desk, broadband internet access, DVD players, full range of international and Chinese television and movie channels, coffee and tea-making facilities, European-style linens, in-room safe, mini bar stocked with European brands of food and drink, hair dryer, ironing board with iron. Some rooms have a circular bathtub which overlooks the lake. The beds have Western style pillow top mattresses. The large bathrooms are well designed with premium amenities. The odd location and theme are a bit strange but the guest rooms are on par with the best. ♦♦♦♦♦

✉ **OCT East, Dameisha,** Yantian
盐田区 东部华侨城

深圳顶级酒店

⑬ The Intertlaken OCT Hotel Shenzhen 深圳茵特拉根华侨城酒店

☎	Phone	+86 755 8888 3333
	Fax	+86 755 8888 3331
	Web	www.interlakenocthotel.com
	Email	rsvn@interlakenocthotel.com
Total Number of Rooms		299
Std. Room Rate		$ $ $ $

Dameisha - Credits 韦洪兴

⑭ Sheraton Dameisha Resort 深圳大梅沙京基喜来登度假酒店

COMPLETED IN 2007, this resort is the first luxury hotel in Shenzhen coastal town of Dameisha. The striking modern architecture resembles a glass dragon overlooking the hotel's private beach on Dapeng Bay. The large lobby is artful and bright with wonderful natural textures under a glass atrium. A fabulous glass chandelier sits above a modern circular feng shui fountain. Small bamboo groves define the comfortable seating area giving the large space a sense of intimacy. The lobby lounge overlooks the huge free form swimming pool that wraps sinuously around the hotel and beach. As one might expect at a resort hotel, the recreation facilities are extensive. There are three outdoor swimming pools with the largest an enormous 1,300 m². Another indoor pool is heated. The fitness center is well equipped with views of the beach. There is an unsupervised kids play area plus a tennis court. The Spring Field Spa features Chinese wellness treatments. The beach area has water sports available from 3rd party operators. Golf is available nearby at Guanlanhu

in the Overseas Chinese Town Holiday Resort. Other nearby attractions include Minsk World, a decommissioned Russian aircraft carrier turned theme park. Oddly except for a sundries shop there are no retail outlets in the hotel which is not convenient as the area is a bit isolated. The outstanding guest rooms all face the ocean with balconies. The smallest rooms, Ocean Deluxe, are a generous 50 m². All rooms have Sheraton Sweet Sleeper beds, 37" flat screen LCD TVs, Safes, voice mail, mini bar, writing desks iron and ironing boards. Broadband Internet is RMB 50 per day. The bathrooms are modern with a large circular bath tub which overlooks the bedroom and ocean beyond. The decorations are contemporary but low key with natural colors. The view of the beach is something special. On the weekends, the Sheraton Dameisha Resort fills its rooms with Shenzhen and Hong Kong residents looking for a luxury escape in a tranquil environment. During the week, it's all business with meeting groups. The resort seems to handle both very well. The distant

14 **Sheraton Dameisha Resort** 深圳大梅沙京基喜来登度假酒店

location may deter international visitors from staying here, but for those	that make the effort they will be surprised and rewarded. ❤❤❤❤❤

✉	9, Yankui Road, Dameisha, Yantian 盐田区大梅沙盐蔡路9号	
✆	Phone Fax Web Email	+86 755 8888 6688 +86 755 8888 1233 www.sheraton.com/dameisha dameisha.sheraton@sheraton.com
Total Number of Rooms	386	
Std. Room Rate		

Xiaomeisha - Credits 韦洪兴

A Day in Shenzhen

A Day in Shenzhen 198

Getting **There** 208

Window of the World - Credits 林琛

主题公园	Theme **Parks**	198
购物	Shopping	200
餐饮 & 夜生活	**Dining** and **Nightlife**	202
文化	Soak up some **Culture**	204
其它活动	Other **Things** to do...	204
地址,公交,地铁站,门票,营业时间,网站	What you need to know to get there: locations, bus numbers, MTR stations, entrance fees, opening hours, websites, etc.	208

A Day in Shenzhen

WHAT TO DO on a Sunday afternoon, or evening, in Shenzhen? Well, that depends on whether you're a visitor or a resident. Those who haven't been here before will probably be seeking something "Chinese-y" so you can take home a few good stories. You will also be more interested in "highlights," and less interested in getting off the beaten path. If you have been here for a while, though, you may be seeking a taste of home, like Western food or mall shopping. On the other hand, having done all the usual things, you may be looking for something a bit more unusual.

The **Theme Parks**

If you have not read anything at all about Shenzhen, you probably know about Window of the World 世界之窗 **1** where you can "see all the world's landmarks in one day." This might appeal more to Chinese citizens, who may not have traveled abroad. World visitors, however, will probably find China Folk Cultural Villages 中国民俗文化村 **2** and Splendid China 锦绣中华 **3** more interesting, where you can see full-sized traditional architecture from twenty-some Chinese minorities, as well as miniatures of most of China's major tourist attractions. Both of these theme parks are easy to

reach near the west end of Metro Line 1 (Window of the World is at Shijie Zhichuang 世界之窗, Splendid China 锦绣中华 and China Folk Cultural Villages 中国民俗文化村 at Huaqiao Cheng 华侨城). Also located at Shijie Zhichuang 世界之窗 is Happy Valley 欢乐谷 **4**, more of a thrill-ride place. This is probably not the best bet for short-timers, but could be good for residents. In addition to the "Big Three Theme Parks," there is a zoo 野生动物园 out in Xili Lake Resort 西丽湖度假村 **5**; again, this is probably better for long-time stays. But for your money, one of Shenzhen's best-kept secrets is the Shenzhen International Botanical Garden 深圳国际园林花卉博览园 **6** (Yuan Boyuan), near Qiaocheng Dong Station 侨城东 on Line 1. At this writing admission is free; the extensive gardens include pavilions, bridges, statuary, and other elements that replicate some of China's most elegant and relaxing places.

> **Verdict**: If you do only one, make it the Shenzhen International Botanical Garden 园博园 **6** (Yuan Boyuan). Second place: China Folk Cultural Villages 中国民俗文化村 **2**, Splendid China 锦绣中华 **3**. Each can be done in a half-day, and are best done in good weather.

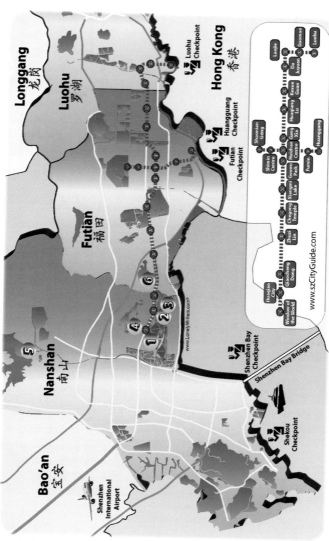

▲ **A day in Shenzhen - Theme parks**

深圳一日游

A DAY IN SHENZHEN

WWW.szCityGuide.com

Shopping

SHENZHEN IS A well-known shopper's Mecca. The "Big Three Shopping areas" are Luohu Commercial City 罗湖商业城 **1**, Dongmen 东门 **2**, and Huaqiang Bei 华强北 **3**.

Luohu Commercial City 罗湖商业城 **1** "LCC" is the granddaddy of them all. With five floors of tightly-packed shops, there is almost nothing you will want that you cannot find, from small electronics to clothes to Tibetan trinkets to tea. It's the focal point for tailored goods in Shenzhen. LCC is at Luohu Metro Station 罗湖站 near the crossing to Hong Kong.

Dongmen 东门 **2** is like a spread-out version of LCC 罗湖商业城 **1**. Evolved from a three-hundred-year-old market, it is still a sort of labyrinth, which can be bewildering. Lots of clothes, arts, and branded shops here, with the emphasis on trendy, youthful things. There are nightclubs and restaurants here too, making it a good place to remain after dark. Laojie Metro Station 老街站.

Huaqiang Bei 华强北 **3** is another place with lots of clothes, though the fashions here tend to be a bit more mature/conservative. More prominent, however, is the electronics business, symbolized by SEG/Saige Tower, Shenzhen's second-tallest building and home to sellers of everything from component parts to finished products. The Huaqiang Bei district

also has quite a few clubs and restaurants. Huaqiang Lu Metro Station 华强路站, exit A.

These three places typify the early phase of Shenzhen's development. In the last few years, upscale malls with shopping, dining, and entertainment (including cinemas, ice-skating, children's play centers, etc.) have sprung up all across the city. Try:

- King Glory Plaza 金光华广场 **4** - Guomao Metro Station 国贸
- The MixC 万象城 **5** - Da Juyuan Station 大剧院站
- Citic Plaza 中信城市广场 **6** - Kexue Guan Station 科学馆站
- Central Walk 中心城 **7** - Huizhan Zhongxin Station 会展中心站
- Coco Park 购物公园 **8** - Gouwu Gongyuan Station 购物公园站
- Garden City 花园城 **9**, Coastal City 海岸城 **10**, and Poly Cultural Center 保利文化广场 **11** - all three off the subway line in central Nanshan; take a cab from Shijie Zhi Chuang Station 世界之窗站 at the west end of Line 1

Verdict: For those short on time, Luohu Commercial City 罗湖商业城 **1** is the place. If you have a whole afternoon, wander around Dongmen shopping streets 东门老街 **2**

深圳一日游

A DAY IN SHENZHEN

www.szCityGuide.com

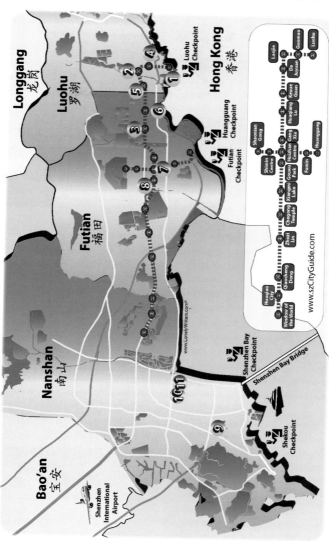

▲ A day in Shenzhen - Shopping

深圳一日游

Dining & **Nightlife**

T**HIS IS A** hugely variable category. What are you after? Clubbing? Bars? Or a quiet meal with good food?

If you're a visitor you will probably want to eat some Chinese food, and there is no shortage of that. The big hotels usually feature excellent meals (though pricey), and generally offer service in English. Note that most hotels serve Cantonese cuisine; this is not surprising as Shenzhen is in Guangdong Province, and "Canton" is a corruption of "Guangdong." In Luohu, try the Shang Palace **1** in the Shangri-la, or Fortune Court **2** in the Crowne Plaza Landmark; in the central area, try the Carrianna **3** in the Marco Polo, or Chiu Chow Garden **4** in the Sheraton Futian; east, El Chino **5** in the Intercontinental, Marco's **6** in the Crowne Plaza "Venice" (at OCT), or Hai Tao **7** in the Kempinski; further down the peninsula, try Donghua Court **8** in the Holiday Inn Donghua, or the Hai Xu Room **9** in the Nanhai Hotel at Shekou.

Of course, there are hundred if not thousands more. If you're truly adventurous, try the street barbecue available late in the evening, but do so at your own risk!

Now for you seeking western food: We cannot begin to tell you everything, but try this: In Luohu, head for the MixC **10** 万象城 - Da Juyuan Station 大剧院站; in the central area, Coco Park **11** 购物公园 - Gouwu Gongyuan Station 购物公园站 and Central Walk **12** 中心城 - Huizhan Zhongxin Station 会展中心站; in northern Nanshan, try Poly Cultural Center 保利文化广场 **13** and Coastal City 海岸城 **14**, or Garden City 花园城 **15**. And for deep Nanshan, hit the Haishang Shijie 海上世界 **16** ("Seaworld Plaza") area in Shekou. By the way, these all have plenty of good Chinese options, too.

Bars? Try a bar street: Renmin Nan area 人民南 **17** at Guomao Station 国贸站, the Citic Plaza 中信城市广场 - Kexue Guan Station 科学馆站 **18** near Kexue Guan Station 科学馆站, the small bar street at Coco Park 购物公园 - Gouwu Gongyuan Station 购物公园站 **19**, Window of the World 世界之窗 **20**, and the aforementioned Seaworld 海上世界 in Shekou **16**.

> **Verdict**: For Chinese, just choose the nearest of the named hotels; for western, Seaworld 海上世界 **16** at Shekou has the most choices; and ditto for Shekou bars.

深圳一日游

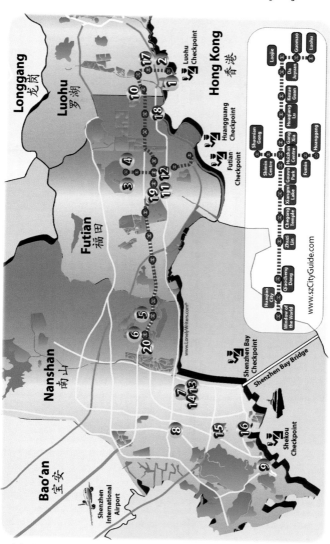

▲ **A day in Shenzhen - Dinning and nightlife**

深圳一日游

Soak Up Some **Culture**

NO MATTER WHAT you've heard, there's plenty of culture to be had in Shenzhen. If you are looking for art, try the Shenzhen Art Museum 深圳美术馆 **1** at the north end of Donghu (Eastlake) Park 东湖公园; the Guan Shanyue Museum 关山月美术馆 **2** in Lianhuashan Park 莲花山公园; or the He Xiangning Art Gallery 何香凝美术馆 **3** in OCT 华侨城 The He Xiangning Museum also sponsors the OCT Contemporary Art Terminal 当代艺术中心 **4** across the street and a long walk to the east. Though it is not a museum, Dafen Village 大芬油画村 **5** in Buji 布吉 is a great place to see and buy art.

Other cultural venues include the Shenzhen Museum 深圳市博物馆 **6** across from Citic Plaza 中信城市广场 - Kexue Guan Station (Kexue Guan Station 科学馆站), and, further out, the Hakka Museum 深圳龙岗客家民俗博物馆 **7** in Longgang Town, Longgang 龙岗区; and the Dapeng Fortress 大鹏古城博物馆 **8** a Ming-period naval fort **9** on the Dapeng Peninsula in south Longgang District. There's an old tower at the base of Bao'an's Phoenix Mountain 宝安区福永凤凰山 **10** and a temple (with grottoes) on the top. You may have to spend an hour on a bus, or hire a car, to see some of these.

Speaking of temples: Hong Fa Temple 弘法寺 in Xian Hu 仙湖植物园 (Fairy Lake) Park **11** is Shenzhen's largest Buddhist temple; there are numerous folk temples scattered throughout the city, including a nice one in the center of Xiasha Village in the south of Futian District.

But for the ultimate "Old Shenzhen" experience, take a walk in an old village area. Try Hubei Village 湖贝旧村 and Luoling 螺岭 **12**, just east of Dongmen; or Xin'an Village 新安村 **13** near Zhongshan Park 中山公园 in Nanshan, which includes a museum.

> **Verdict**: The five-storey Shenzhen Museum has a little bit of everything: history, natural history, fine arts. It's a wonderful jumble of "all things Shenzhen," and fills up a good afternoon.

Other **Things to Do**

SHENZHEN IS BLESSED with dozens of parks, large and small. Our favorite is Lizhi 荔枝公园 (Litchi or Lychee) Park **1** at the intersection of Shennan and Hongling Roads (Da Juyuan Station 大剧院站 Exit B). Here on a Sunday afternoon you will find Chinese folk doing Chinese things: playing Chinese chess, practicing musical instruments, doing Taijiquan 太极拳 (aka Taichi), all these and more. If you rather do than watch, head for Lianhuashan 莲

深圳一日游

A DAY IN SHENZHEN

www.SzCityGuide.com

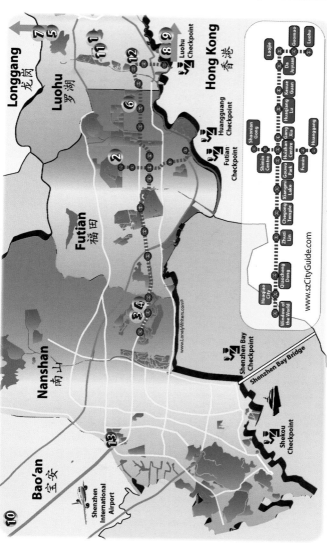

www.LonelyWriters.com®

www.SzCityGuide.com

▲ **A day in Shenzhen - Culture**

花山公园 (Lotus Mountain) Park **2** and take a walk up to the statue of Deng Xiaoping at the top of the hill, where there's an excellent view of the city center. Or buy a kite near the southeast entrance and fly it in the Kite Square. More ambitious view-seekers might "climb" Nanshan 南山 **3**, the mountain just north of Shekou in Nanshan District. By all accounts it's more of an uphill walk than a climb. For more strenuous climbs check out Mount Wutong 梧桐山 **4** and Mount Maluan 马峦山郊野公园 **5** in the east, and Yangtai Mountain 深圳羊台山 **6** in Bao'an, just north of Xili in Nanshan.

How about a magnificent view with no effort? Try the View Deck **7** at the top of the Diwang Building 地王大厦 (Da Juyuan Station 大剧院站).

Shenzhen has several excellent golf courses, including Mission Hills **8**, "the largest golf course in the world" with 216 holes. You can ice skate at Poly Cultural Plaza **9** or The MixC 万象城 - Da Juyuan Station 大剧院站 **10**, and even ski at Window of the World 世界之窗 **11**! Like it warmer? Head for the Eastern beaches of Dameisha 大梅沙 or Xiaomeisha 小梅沙 **12**, or head out to the even more remote Nan'ao area, including Xichong beach 西冲(西涌)三门岛 **13**. Want to pamper yourself? Shenzhen abounds in spas, foot massage shops, and more. If you want to stay on the safe side, try Queen Spa

14 on Chunfeng Road just north of Dongmen South Road. All you'd expect - sauna, whirlpool, massage, and so on - and a few surprises, such as a water slide, bubble bath, ping-pong, snooker, and a mini-cinema.

Verdict: If you have time for just one more thing, after all of the above, it would be this: Take a stroll through the center of town. Starting at Central Walk 中心城 **15** (or even as far south as the Exhibition Center, Huizhan Zhongxin 会展中心), head north. You will go through a small park, then cross under Shennan to reach City Hall. Keep going and you'll be between the Children's Palace **16** on the right and Book City (worth an hour) on the left. Go past Book City to the left and see the Library and Concert Hall. (Locals: There are dozens of English magazines on the 5th floor of the Library.) Your walk ends at Lianhuashan **2** (mentioned above); you can get on the train at Shaonian Gong 少年宫 (Children's Palace) Station to head home. Well, that should keep you busy for a while. If you've done all of the above, you can really say you've "done Shenzhen."

■ Brought to you by
James Baquet
www.ShenzhenBuzz.com

深圳一日游

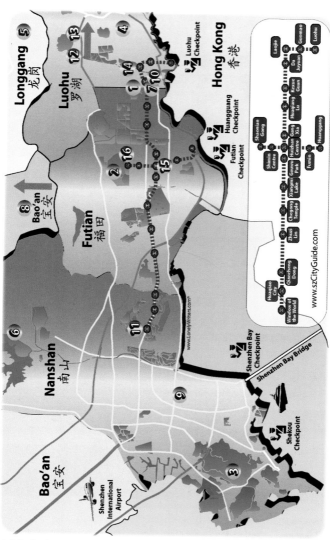

▲ A day in Shenzhen - Other things to do

深圳一日游

Getting **There**

1- The Theme Parks

① **Window of the World** 世界之窗

✉	南山区华侨城 Overseas Chinese Town, Nanshan
☎	+86 755 2660 8000
🚌	Bus: 70, 113, 324, 328, 329, 370 MTR: Window of the World Station, Shijie Zhichuang Station - 世界之窗站
⏳	9am - 9:30pm
$	120RMB
🖱	www.szwwco.com

② **China Folk Cultural Villages** 中国民俗文化村

✉	Overseas Chinese Town, Nanshan 南山区华侨城
☎	+86 755 2660 6526
🚌	Bus: 101,204, 209, 223, 301 MTR: Huaqiao Cheng Station - 华侨城站
⏳	9am - 9pm
$	120RMB
🖱	http://www.cn5000.com.cn/english/about/index.asp

③ **Splendid China** 锦绣中华

✉	Overseas Chinese Town, Nanshan 南山区华侨城
☎	+86 755 2660 6526
🚌	Bus: 101,204, 209, 223, 301 MTR: Huaqiao Cheng Station - 华侨城站
⏳	9am - 9pm
$	120RMB

③ Splendid China 锦绣中华

🖰	http://www.cn5000.com.cn/english/about/index.asp

④ Happy Valley 欢乐谷

✉	Overseas Chinese Town, Nanshan 南山区华侨城
☎	+86 755 2690 1309
🚌	Bus: 70, 113, 324, 328, 329, 370 MTR: Shijie Zhichuang Station - 世界之窗站
⧗	9:30am - 10pm
$	140RMB
🖰	www.happyvalley.com.cn

⑤ Xili Lake Resort 西丽湖度假村

✉	Xili Zhen, Nanshan 南山区西丽镇
☎	+86 755 2651 1350, 2651 1366
🚌	Bus: 442, 101 from train station 火车站 Bus: 434 from Splendid China 锦绣中华 Bus: 435 from Nantou Bus Station 南头车站
⧗	8am - 10pm
$	Free

⑤ Shenzhen Zoo 野生动物园

✉	Eastern Part of Xili Lake, Nanshan 南山区西丽湖东侧
☎	+86 755 266 22888
🚌	Bus: 101,104,240, 226, 361, 66
⧗	8:30am - 6pm
$	120RMB
🖰	www.szzoo.net

6 **International Botanical Garden** 深圳国际园林花卉博览园

✉	Zhuzilin Xi,Futian 福田区竹子林西
☎	+86 755 **8282 9075 / 8282 9085**
🚌	Bus: 104, 105, 107, 108, 109 MTR: Qiaocheng Dong Station - 桥城东站
⏳	9am - 8pm
$	Free
🖰	www.szyby.cn

2- Soak Up Some **Culture**

1 **Shenzhen Art Museum** 深圳美术馆

✉	Inside East Lake Park, Aiguo Road, Luohu 罗湖区爱国路东湖公园内
☎	+86 755 **2542 6069**
🚌	Bus: 3, 17, 365, 351, 336, 29 get off at Reservoir, Shuiku 水库
⏳	Daily: 9am - 5pm Closed on Monday
$	5RMB Free admission on Fridays
🖰	www.szam.org

1 **Donghu (Eastlake) Park** 东湖公园

✉	11, Road 1, Aiguo Donglu, Luohu 罗湖区爱国路一街11号
☎	+86 755 **2542 9205, 2541 0719**
🚌	Bus: 3, 17, 29 get of at Reservoir, Shuiku 水库
⏳	8am - 10pm
$	Free

❷ Guan Shanyue Museum　　　关山月美术馆

✉	6026, Hongli Road, Futian 福田区红荔路6026号
✆	+86 755 8306 3086
🚌	Bus: 10, 25, 105, 215, 111 MTR: Shaonian Gong Station Exit B - 少年宫站 B 出口
⏳	Daily: 9am - 5pm Closed on Mondays
$	10RMB Free admission on Fridays
🖱	www.gsyart.com

❸ He Xiangning Art Gallery　　　何香凝美术馆

✉	Overseas Chinese Town, Shennan Road, Nanshan 南山区深南路华侨城
✆	+86 755 2660 4540
🚌	Bus: 26, 101, 105, 113, 204 MTR: Huaqiao Cheng Station - 华侨城站
⏳	Tuesday-Sunday, 10am - 5:30pm Closed on Mondays
$	20RMB Free admission on Fridays
🖱	www.hxnart.com

❹ OCT Contemporary Art Terminal　　　当代艺术中心

✉	En Ping Road, Overseas Chinese Town 南山区华侨城恩平路
✆	+86 755 2691 5100
🚌	Bus: 101, 113, 21, 319, 338, 105, get off at 康佳集团东 Kangjia Jituan Dong MTR: Qiaocheng Dong Station Exit A - 侨城东站 A 出口
⏳	Tuesday-Sunday: 10am - 5:30pm Closed on Mondays
$	Free
🖱	www.ocat.com.cn

4 OCT   华侨城

✉	Overseas Chinese Town, Nanshan 南山区华侨城
☏	NA
🚌	Bus: 101, 204, 209, 223, 301 MTR: Huaqiao Cheng Station - 华侨城站
⌛	NA
$	NA
🖱	NA

5 Dafen Village in Buji   大芬油画村

✉	Buji Street, Longgang 龙岗区布吉街道
☏	+86 755 8473 2633
🚌	Bus: 512, 863, 616, 537, 315, 66
⌛	NA
$	NA
🖱	www.cndafen.com dafenop@126.com

6 Shenzhen Museum   深圳市博物馆

✉	1008 Shennan Road Central, Futian 福田区深南中路1008号
☏	+86 755 8210 1706
🚌	Bus: 3, 8, 12, 101, 113, 204, 215 MTR: Da Juyuan Station - 大剧院站
⌛	Daily: 10 am - 5pm Closed on Mondays
$	10RMB 5RMB for Students Free admission on Fridays
🖱	NA

❼ Hakka Museum 龙岗客家民俗博物馆

✉	1, Luoruihe North Street, Longgang Street, Longgang 龙岗区龙岗街道罗瑞合北街一号
☎	+86 755 2883 5108
🚌	Bus: 365, 351, 329
⏳	8am - 11:30am 2pm - 5pm
$	10RMB
🖱	NA

❽ Dapeng Fortress 大鹏古城博物馆

✉	Pengcheng Community, Dapeng Street, Longgang 龙岗区大鹏街道鹏城社区
☎	+86 755 8431 9269
🚌	Bus: 364, 360, 833, 818
⏳	Daily: 8:30am - 6 pm
$	20RMB
🖱	www.szdpsc.com

❿ Fenghuang Temple 宝安区福永凤凰山

✉	Fenghuang Cun,Fuyong Zhen,Bao'an 宝安区福永镇凤凰村
☎	NA
🚌	Bus: 310-315 Circle Line 环线 from Window of the World Station 世界之窗站 to Tongfuyu Gongyequ 同富裕工业区, then change bus to No.754
⏳	NA
$	Free
🖱	NA

⑪ Hong Fa Temple

弘法寺 / 仙湖植物园

✉	Shenzhen Fairy Lake Botanical Garden, No. 160, Xianhu Lu, Luohu 罗湖区仙湖路160号仙湖植物园
☎	+86 755 2573 8430
🚌	Bus: 57, 65, 218, 220, 382
⏳	6am - 11pm
$	20RMB Children 1.1 ~ 1.4m tall:10RMB
🖱	http://www.szbg.org/English%20web/main.htm

⑫ Luoling

螺岭

✉	Wenjin Road Central, Luohu 罗湖区文锦中路
☎	NA
🚌	Bus: 2, 27, 40, 111, 242
⏳	NA
$	NA
🖱	NA

⑫ Hubei Village

湖贝旧村

✉	Hubei Road, Luohu 罗湖区湖贝路
☎	NA
🚌	Bus: 2,10,17,29,56 Get off at Guangshen Binguan 广深宾馆
⏳	NA
$	NA
🖱	NA

深圳一日游

A DAY IN SHENZHEN

www.szCityGuide.com

13 Xin'an Village 新安村 / 中山公园

✉	Beside Nantou Footbridge, Nanshan District 南山区南头天桥旁
✆	NA
🚌	Bus: 201,204,210,226,227
⏳	NA
$	NA
🖱	NA

3- Other **Things to Do**

1 Lizhi (Lychee) Park 荔枝公园

✉	Hongling Zhonglu,Futian 福田区红岭中路
✆	+86 755 8209 5655
🚌	Bus: 10, 13, 24, 30, 105, 202, 228
⏳	5:30am -11pm
$	Free
🖱	NA

2 Lianhuashan Park 莲花山公园

✉	Hongli Xilu,Futian 福田区红荔西路
✆	NA
🚌	Bus: 25, 105, 228, 215, 15, 111
⏳	8am - 10pm
$	Free
🖱	NA .

③ Nanshan (Mountain) 大南山

✉	At the corner of Dongbin Rd. and Nanhai Ave., Nanshan 南山区东滨路与南海大道交界
✆	+86 755 2682 7910
🚌	Bus: 70; get off at Lianhe Yiyuan 联合医院 Bus: 226; get off at 海上世界Seaworld Bus: 113; get off at 海洋大厦 Haiyan Dasha
⌛	6am - 7pm
$	Free
🖱	NA

④ Mount Wutong 梧桐山

✉	Dawang Cun, Shawan, Luohu 罗湖区沙湾大旺村
✆	+86 755 2571 0396
🚌	Bus: 103, 202, 205, 220, 218, 113
⌛	8am - 7pm
$	Free
🖱	NA

⑤ Mount Maluan 马峦山郊野公园

✉	Mount Maluan, Pingshan Zhen, Longgang 龙岗区坪山镇马峦山
✆	+86 755 8978 5020
🚌	Bus: 103, 360, 364, 380 Get off at Xiaomeisha 小梅沙
⌛	24 hours
$	Free
🖱	NA

深圳一日游

A DAY IN SHENZHEN

www.szCityGuide.com

6 Yangtai Mountain in Bao'an 深圳羊台山

✉	宝安区石岩镇 Shiyanzhen,Baoan
☏	+86 755 2752 2408
🚌	Bus: 325 from Gangxia 岗夏 to Shiyan Bus Station 石岩汽车站, then change bus to No. 769 to Yangtaishan terminal 羊台山总站
⏳	Closes at 6pm
$	Free
🖱	NA

7 Diwang Building 地王大厦

✉	Diwang Dasha,Shennan Zhonglu, Luohu 罗湖区深南中路地王大厦
☏	+86 755 8246 3789
🚌	Bus: 101,10,233 MTR: Da Juyuan Station Exit D - 大剧院站 D出口
⏳	8:30am - 11pm
$	Sightseeing on the top of Diwang: 60RMB
🖱	NA

8 Mission Hills Golf Course 深圳观澜球会

✉	No1,Guanlan Golf Ave., Bao'an 宝安区观澜高尔夫大道1号
☏	+86 755 2802 0888
🚌	Bus: 312, 770, 771, 793; get off at Gaoerfu Qiuchang 高尔夫球场
⏳	8am - 10pm To play golf you should either be a member or stay in the hotel. Weekdays price: 1320RMB. Sunday and holiday surcharge applies, call for prices
🖱	www.missionhillsgroup.com

(12) **Dameisha**		大梅沙
✉	Dameisha,Yantian 盐田区大梅沙	
☏	+86 755 5062323	
🚌	Bus: 53, 103, 239, 242	
⏳	24 hours	
$	Free	
🖱	NA	

(12) **Xiaomeisha**		小梅沙
✉	East of Dapeng Bay, Yantian 盐田区东部大鹏海湾	
☏	+86 755 25035999 - 8815	
🚌	Bus: 103, 360, 364, 380	
⏳	10am - 7pm Peak season: 9:30am - 0:30am	
$	20RMB	
🖱	www.szxms.com.cn	

(13) **Zhongshan Park**		中山公园
✉	No. 42,Zhongshan Xijie,Jiu Jie,Nanshan 南山区九街中山西街42号	
☏	+86 755 2661 2335	
🚌	Bus: 2, 27, 40, 111, 242	
⏳	6:00am - 10:00pm	
$	Free	
🖱	NA	

深圳一日游

A DAY IN SHENZHEN

www.szCityGuide.com

Mount Wutong - Credits 韦洪兴

Splendid Shenzhen

👁 Old & New Shenzhen	Civic Center	👁
👁 Window of the World	Dameisha & Xiaomesha	👁
👁 Splendid China, Cultural Folk Village, & Happy Valley	Exhibition Center	👁
👁 Diwang Sightseeing Building	Bao'an	👁
👁 Nanshan & Shekou	Diwang & SEG Sightseeing Buildings	👁
👁 Dongmen	Shenzhen Zoo at night	👁
👁 Xianhu & Lianhua Shan Parks	Shenzhen Bay Bridge	👁
👁 Lizhi Park	Tibetan Dance at Baoli Theater, Nanshan	👁

WE HAD BEEN searching for the past 2 months a photographer who had captured Shenzhen's scenery. "There must be someone who has been taking Shenzhen's best spots!" I argued with my friends. Back then, we had been able to find students willing to travel Shenzhen to take pictures, but with the weather conditions we had, they wouldn't look as good as I wanted them to be.

Reading this, you must be thinking: "Is there something to see in Shenzhen?", or "Shenzhen is a relatively young city, there is nothing to see!" After meeting with Mr. Wei, if I still had doubts on that matter, my vision of Shenzhen changed forever.

The photographer who took the pictures displayed in this chapter, "Splendid Shenzhen", is not only a professional photographer but also one Shenzhen's most famous photographers. If you Google or Baidu (www. baidu.com, China's most popular web search engine) his name, it will return thousands of hits. Mr. Wei Hongxing 韦洪兴 is a 70-year old man who has been capturing Shenzhen's scenery since 1980. "Every year I go to the same places to shoot the same scenery. Even after almost 30 years, each time it's a new experience to me" said Mr. Wei with a sparkle in his eyes.

His pictures have been displayed in Shenzhen's most beautiful books, magazines, posters, and postcards.

If you happen to go to Book City 书城, ask the staff to guide you to the Shenzhen postcards section, then check out the photographer's name on the back of them; most probably you'll see: "韦洪兴". For those who work for, or with, the Shenzhen Government, you certainly have had the opportunity to see his work in several "private" collections, distributed to foreign and Chinese officials. If you have the chance to know Mr. Wei or to work with him, you might even see yourself offered a set of these fantastic Shenzhen books and posters.

Mr. Wei has thousands of pictures on display on his website: www.sztp8. com. Choosing which ones to present in this book wasn't an easy task. After a long while browsing through landscapes and scenery, we planned on showing not less than 20 places, selected from Shenzhen's 6 districts. That still does not cover all areas in Shenzhen, however. We originally selected more than 50 places, but because of some space and time constraints, we picked up the places that most people coming to and living in Shenzhen would be likely to go.

I really hope you will enjoy Mr. Wei's photographs as much as we did when we first saw them.

■ Brought to you by
Adriano Lucchese 唐毅德
www.LonelyWriters.com 瓏玲作家

Old and **New Shenzhen**

▶ 2000

▶ 1983

▲ **Shennan Central Road**

▶ Huangjiang Bei 1983-2005

深圳过去与现在

SPLENDID SHENZHEN

华强北路　　女人世界　　深南中路东

Huaqiang Bei　　▲ Women's World　　▲ East Shennan Central Road

2005

1983

Old & New Shenzhen - Credits 韦洪兴

Window of the **World**

世界之窗

Windows of the World - Credits 韦洪兴

Splendid China, Cultural Folk **Villages**, & **Happy Vall**

锦绣中华，中国民俗文化村，欢乐谷

Splendid China, Cultural Folk Village, & Happy Valley - Credits 韦洪兴

Diwang Sightseeing Building

地王大厦

Diwang Sightseeing Building - Credits 韦洪兴

Nanshan & Shekou

南山、蛇口

Nanshan & Shekou - Credits 韦洪兴

Dongmen

东门

Dongmen - Credits 韦洪兴

Xianhu & **Lianhua Shan** Parks

仙湖植物园、莲花山公园

SPLENDID SHENZHEN

Xianhu & Lianhua Shan Parks - Credits 韦洪兴

Lizhi Park

荔枝公园

Lizhi Park - Credits 韦洪兴

Civic Center

市民中心

Civic Center - Credits 韦洪兴

Dameisha & Xiaomeisha

大梅沙，小梅沙

Dameisha & Xiaomeisha - Credits 韦洪兴

Exhibition Center

会展中心

Exhibition Center - Credits 韦洪兴

Bao'an

宝安区

Bao'an - Credits 韦洪兴

Diwang & **SEG(Saige)** Sightseeing Buildings

Diwang Sightseeing Building - Credits 韦洪兴

Splendid Shenzhen

地王、赛格观光

SEG(Saige) Sightseeing Building - Credits 韦洪兴

Shenzhen Zoo at night

深圳动物园夜景

Shenzhen Zoo at night - Credits 韦洪兴

Shenzhen **Bay Bridge**

深圳湾大桥

Shekou Bay Bridge - Credits 韦洪兴

Tibetan Dance at Baoli Theater, Nanshan

藏族舞, 南山保利大剧院

Tibetan Dance at Baoli theater - Credits 韦洪兴

Index

0-9

2nd hand Computers 80
2nd hand Market 93
2nd hand Printers 74
4 Dragons Home 112

A

Adidas 110
Airports
    Hong Kong International Airport
        125
    Shenzhen International Airport
        105
Antiques 120
    Exporting Antiques 121
Apple Stores 78, 110
Armani 108
Art Gallery
    He Xiangning Art Gallery 211
    OCT Contemporary Art Terminal
        211
Artificial flowers 118
Arts 11, 13, 16, 20, 23, 58
    Baoli theatre 106
Arts, Museums & Temples
    Boya Arts City 58
    Dafen Village in Buji 212
    Dapeng Fortress 213
    Fengshan Temple 213
    Guan Shanyue Museum 211
    Hakka Museum 213
    He Xiangning Art Gallery 211
    Hongfa Temple 214
    Hongji Handicraft City 59
    OCT Contemporary Art Terminal
        211
    Shenzhen Art Museum 210
    Shenzhen Museum 212

B

Baby Car Seats 89
Baby Monitors 86
Baima Fabric Market 53
Baima Olympic Market 55
Bao'an 244
Bao'an Phoenix Mountain 204, 213
Baohua Lou 51
Baoli Poly Cultural Theater 106,
        252
Beaches
    Dameisha 218
    Xiaomeisha 218
    Xichong 218
Beauty 13, 16, 20, 60, 61, 90, 91, 92
Beddings 56, 60
Belts 19, 55
Blue Jeans & T-shirts 11, 13, 15, 19
Book City
    Futian 105
    Nanshan 106
Books 93, 103
Boya Arts City 58
B&Q 105, 111, 115
Broidery 55
Buji Village 204

C

Cacharel 110
Caps & Hats 20
CAQ (Kitchen Equipment) 63, 117
Car Radio/CD Sets 84
Carrefour 102, 106
Carving 58
Cashmere & Pashmina
        13, 16, 20, 23
Casual Wear 91
CD 103, 123
Central Walk 102, 200, 202
Cerruti 108
Chanel 62, 67

Chargers 84
Children Books 89
Children's Palace 206
Children's Wear 11, 13, 15, 20
Children's World 89
China Cultural Folk Villages 198, 208
Chinaware 112
Chinese Corner 128
Chinese Dictionary 145
Chinese Paintings 58
Chinese Vases 58
Cinemas 60, 98, 100, 102, 110
CITIC Plaza 200, 202
Civic Center 238
Clothes 11, 13, 15, 19, 23, 90, 93, 122
   Chinese Traditional 13, 15, 20
   Golf 15, 20
   Men's Fashion 19
   Men's Ties 13
   Women's Fashion 15, 19
Clothes - big sizes 93
Coastal City 105, 106, 202
Coco Park 101, 200, 202
Communication Equipment 84
Computer Desktops 74
Computer Hardware 68
Computer Peripherals 68
Computers 68, 109
Converse 60
Cosmetics 61, 90, 91, 92
Costal City 106
Craft Work 112
Crocs 60
Croissants de France 60
Crowne Plaza Hotel OCT 202
Crowne Plaza Landmark Hotel 202
Crystal Decoration 55, 94
Cuisine 146–173
   Chef Martin Yan 147–151
Culture Square - Dongmen 42
Curtain Fabric 16, 55, 56

D

Dafen Village 204, 212
Dameisha 206, 218, 240
Dapeng Fortress 204, 213
Decathlon 111
Diamonds 94, 119
Digital cameras 68
Digital equipment 61, 68
Dior 67
Diwang Sightseeing Building 206, 217, 228, 246
Dongguan 122, 125
Donghu (Eastlake) Park 204, 210
Dongmen 42–65, 200, 232
Dongmen Fabric and Curtain Market 56, 57
Dongmen Shoe City 50
Duty Free 94
Duty Free Jewelry 94
DVD 123
DVD players 83, 84
DYI Computers 74

E

Electrical Appliances 61
Electronic Components 76, 77
Emerald 94
English Books 103
European City 105, 111
Exhibition Center 102, 242
Eye Glasses 16, 59, 90

F

Fabric 11, 16, 23, 54
Fabric places in Dongmen 57
Fairy Lake 204
Fashion 16, 26, 90, 91, 92, 93, 98, 99, 100, 101, 102, 109, 110, 120, 122
Ferry 6, 105
Films 103
Fitness Equipment 61

Flowers 112
Foot Massage 56
Foreign Clothing Market 93
Four Dragons Home 112
Frames 55, 58
Furniture 91, 112, 113, 122
  Jinhui in Nanshan 105
Furniture - classical 112
Furniture Factories 122
Furniture Street 122
Futian Stationery Mall 118

G

Gaiwan Tea 39
Garden City 105, 110, 200
Genryoku Sushi 110
Geox 110
Gold 94
Golf
  Mission Hills Golf Course 191,
    217
Gome Electronics 79, 85
Guangzhou 125
Guan Shanyue Museum 211

H

Haagen Daaz 90
Hair accessories 118
Hair Salon 56
Haiya Department Store 105, 106
Hakka Museum 204, 213
Handbags 11, 13, 15, 19, 92, 123
Happy Valley 198, 209
Herbal Products 56
He Xiangning Art Gallery 204, 211
Hi-fi 68, 83
HOBA Home Furnishings 114
Holiday Plaza 105, 109
Holpe Mobile Phone 82
Home Appliances 62, 106, 111,
    112, 113, 114, 116, 117
Home Décor 112
Home Designers 112

Home Furnishings 113, 114, 115
Home Furnishings & DIY 115
Home Ornament 61, 112
Home Theater 68, 83
Hongfa Temple 204, 214
Hongji Handicraft City 59
Hong Kong 105
Hotel Furniture 116
Hotels 174–195
  Bao'an
    Mission Hills Resort 191
  Dongmen
    Metropole Hotel 64
  Futian
    Four Points by Sheraton Shen-
      zhen 188
    Marco Polo Shenzhen 189
    Sheraton Shenzhen Futian
      190
  Luohu
    Crowne Plaza Hotel & Suites
      Landmark Shenzhen 178
    Shangri-La Hotel Shenzhen
      179
  Nanshan
    Crowne Plaza Shenzhen 180
    Cruise Inn Hotel Shenzhen
      181
    Fraser Place Shekou 182
    Inter-Continental Shenzhen
      183
    Kempinski Hotel Shenzhen
      185
    Nan Hai Hotel 187
  Yantian
    Sheraton Dameisha Resort
      194
    The Intertlaken OCT Hotel
      Shenzhen 192
Houjie Street 122
Household Furnishings 20, 91
Huaqiang Bei 66–95, 200
Huaqiang Electronics Plaza 77
Huaqiang Electronics World 76

Hubei Village 204, 214
Hugo Boss 108
Huibao Kitchen Equipment 116, 117
Huizhou 125
Humen City 122

I

Ice Skating Rink 98
Ikea 111, 116
Illy Coffee 102
Intercontinental Hotel 202
International Electronics Market 84
International Fabric Market 123
Italian Best Coffee 102
iTell Mobile Phone 82

J

Jade 59, 119
Jewelry 13, 16, 20, 53, 61, 94, 119, 121
   Chow Tai Fook jewelry 110
Jewelry Repair Center 94
Jiangmen 125
Jusco 99, 106

K

Kempinski Hotel 106, 202
KFC 44
King Glory Plaza 100, 200
Kitchen Equipment 60, 61, 63, 112, 116, 117
Konka (Brand) 80
Kowloon City Shopping Centre 48

L

Lamp Amplifiers 83
Laptop 74
LCD TV 83
Leather 19, 90, 123
Leisure Clothing 61

Lianhua Shan Park 204, 215, 234
Lierac 110
Living in Shenzhen 262
Lizhi Park 204, 215, 236
L'Oreal 110
Luggage 61
Luohu Commercial City 8–37, 200
Luohu Stationery Malls 118
Luoling 214

M

Macao 125
MAC (Cosmetics) 67
MacDonald's 38, 42
Mango 110
Maps
   Costal City 106
   Dinning and nightlife - A day in Shenzhen 203
   Dongmen 3D Shopping map 44
   From Luohu to Dongmen 43
   Huaqiang Bei 3D Shopping map 70
   Huaqiang Bei quick shopping advice table 68
   Nanshan Shopping map 104
   Other things to do - A day in Shenzhen 207
   Shenzhen Essential 6
   Shenzhen's Best Hotels 177
   Shopping along the MTR line 97
   Shopping Places - A day in Shenzhen 201
   Soak up some culture - A day in Shenzhen 205
   Theme parks - A day in Shenzhen 199
   The Shenzhen Food Guide 153
   Zhuhai, Zhongshan, Macao, Hong Kong, Guangzhou... 125
Marco Polo Hotel 202
Massage 40
Maternity 90

Mc Cormick Spices 60, 111
Men's Clothing 90
Metropole Hotel 64
Metro Supermarket 111
Mission Hills Golf Course 191, 206, 217
MixC Shopping Mall 200, 202, 206
Mobile Phones & Accessories 68, 79, 80, 82, 84, 85
MOI Department Store 43, 62, 67, 91
Mountains
  Mount Maluan 216
  Mount Wutong 216
  Nanshan 216
  Yangtai Mountain in Bao'an 217
Mount Maluan 206, 216
Mount Wutong 206, 216
MP3 76, 77, 79, 84, 85
MP4 76, 77, 79, 84, 85
MTR 96
Museums
  Guan Shanyue Museum 211
  Hakka Museum 213
  Shenzhen Art Museum 210
  Shenzhen Museum 212
Musical Instruments 58, 89, 91
  Parson Music 91

N

Nanhai Hotel 202
Nanshan 105, 230
Nanshan (Mountain) 206, 216
Nantang 52
New Women's City 49
Nico Women's World Fashion Plaza 90
Nike 110
Nikon 75
Norway Oslo 101

O

OCT 204, 212

OCT Contemporary Art Terminal 204, 211
Office Equipment 61
Ole Supermarket 98
Omega Boutique 100
Outerwear 15, 20

P

Paintings 58, 121
Papa John's 44, 106, 110
Park'n Shop 44, 60
Parks
  Donghu (Eastlake) Park 210
  Lianhuashan Park 215
  Lizhi Lychee Park 215
  Zhongshan Park 218
Parson Music 91
PDA 81
Pearl 94, 119
Pharmacy 61
Piaubert 110
Pizza Hut 44, 99
Platinum 94
Poly Cultural Center 106, 200, 202, 206
Porcelain 63, 121
Protection 68, 86
Puma 60
Pyjamas 90

Q

Queen Spa 206

R

Rainbow Department Store 61, 106
Restaurant equipment 63
Restaurants
  Chinese Food
    Meiluxan 169
    Sanshisan Jiantang 165
    Shanxi Hanji 167
    Sichuan Douhua 168

Xiangmixuan 170
Zhongfayuan 166
Indian Food
Bombay Indian Cuisine & Bar 159
Korean Food
Arirang 158
Xiaobaidu BBQ 163
Latin Food
Latin Grillhouse 157
Luohu Commercial City 11, 13, 16, 20, 23
Malaysian Food
Hanglipo Malaysian Fine Cuisine 154
Seafood
Jurenye 164
Tex-Mex
Amigos 155
Vegetarian
Jinhaige 162
Western Food
92 Degrees 161
Ihope Cafe 156
NYPD Pizza 160
Ribbons & Ropes 55
Roller blades 89

S

Saibo Digital Plaza 78
Saige Electronics 104, 105
Saige (SEG) Computer Market 73, 74
Saige (SEG) Digital Market 75
Sculpture 58, 59
Seaworld 105, 202
Security 68, 86
SEG Sightseeing Building 246
Seibu 99
Sephora 108
Sewing Accessories 61
Shangri-la Hotel 202
Shanyue Museum 204
Shekou 105, 202, 230

Shenzhen Art Museum 204, 210
Shenzhen Bay Bridge 105
Shenzhen Book City 103
Shenzhen Daily 267
Shenzhen International Botanical Garden 198, 210
Shenzhen Museum 204, 212
Shenzhen University 105
Shenzhen Zoo 198, 209, 248
Sheraton Futian Hotel 202
Shoes 11, 13, 15, 19
Casual Shoes 19
Chinese Style Shoes 13
Dancing Shoes 15, 19
Men's Shoes 15
Men & Women Shoes 13, 15, 19
Smart Shoes 19
Sport Shoes 15
Shoes factory 123
Shopping Centers
Baima Fabric Market 53, 55
Baohua Lou Dongmen 51
Boya Arts Center 58
B&Q 115
CAQ (Kitchen Equipment) 63, 117
Central Walk 102
Children's World 89
Coco Park 101
Costal City 106
Dongmen Fabric and Curtain Market 56, 57
Dongmen Shoe City 50
Duty Free Jewelry 94
European City 111
Foreign Clothing Trade Market 93
Four Dragons Home 112
Garden City 110
Gome Electronics 79, 85
HOBA Home Furnishings 114
Holiday Plaza 109
Holpe Mobile Phone 82
Hongji Handicraft Centre 59

索引

Huaqiang Electronics Plaza 77
Huaqiang Electronics World 76
Huibao Kitchen Equipment 116, 117
International Electronics Market 84
iTell Mobile Phone 82
King Glory Plaza 100
Kowloon City Shopping Centre 48
Luohu Commercial Center 8
Luohu Stationary Malls 118
MOI Shopping Center 62, 91
Nantang & Zhongwei 52
New Women's City 49
Nico Women's World Fashion Plaza 90
Rainbow Department Store 61
Saibo Digital Plaza 78
Saige (SEG) Computer Market 73, 74
Saige (SEG) Digital Market 75
Shenzhen Book City 103
Spring City Plaza 109
Sundan Electronics 85
Sungang Furniture City 113
Suning Electronics 79, 85
Sun Plaza 60
Tea World 39
The Pacific Protection & Security Market 86
Wanshang Computer City 83
Watch City 87
Women's World 92
Xieheng Mobile Phone 82
Xihua Shopping Palace 51
Yuanwang Digital Mall 81
Silk 26
Silver 94
SK-II 62
Socks 15, 20
Sofa Sets 56, 123
Solomon Store 100
Sono Equipment 83

Souvenirs 126
Spaghetti House 98
Splendid China 198, 208
Sportswear 60, 61, 91
Spring City Plaza 109
Starbucks 44, 60, 91, 98, 99, 102
Stationery 61, 89, 118
Strollers 89
Subway Sandwiches 102
Sundan Electronics 79, 85, 106, 111
Sungang Furniture City 113
Suning Electronics 79, 85
Sun Plaza 60
Supermarkets 61, 62

T

Tablecloths 56
Taco Bell 98
Tailors 23
Tea 23, 38
Teawear 58, 59
Tea World 39
Temples
    Fengshan Temple 213
    Hongfa Temple 214
Theme Parks
    China Folk Cultural Villages 208
    Happy Valley 209
    International Botanical Garden 210
    Shenzhen Zoo 209
    Splendid China 208
    Window of the World 208
    Xili Lake Resort 209
The Pacific Protection & Security Market 86
Ties 55
Towels 20
Toys 11, 75, 89, 118
TV 84
TV cabinet 121

U

Umbrella 92
Underwear 13, 15, 19, 61, 91, 92

V

Vases 59
Video games 84
Villages
    Dafen Village in Buji 212
    Hubei Village 214
    Xin'an Village 215

W

Wanshang Computer City 83
Watch 60, 61, 87, 90, 94, 123
Watch City 87
Wedding 90
Window of the World 198, 208, 224
Wine 61
Women's World 90, 92
Wrangler 110

X

Xianhu Park 234
Xiaomeisha 206, 218, 240
Xiasha Village 204
Xibu Electronics 105
Xichong beach 206
Xieheng Mobile Phone 82
Xihua Shopping Palace 51
Xili Lake Resort 198, 209
Xin'an Village 204, 215

Y

Yamaha Music 83
Yangtai Mountain 206, 217
Yuanwang Digital Mall 81

Z

Zara 108

Zhaoqing 125
Zhongshan City 120, 125
Zhongshan Park 204, 218
Zhongwei 52
Zhuhai 120, 125
ZTC Mobile Phone 80

索引

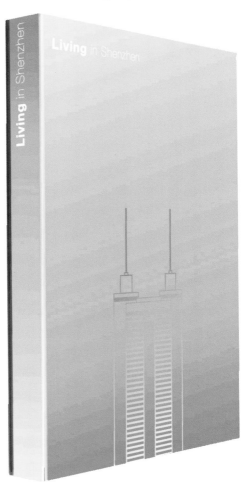

Don't miss **Living** in Shenzhen
Coming up soon!

www.**szCityGuide**.com

Arts in Shenzhen

深圳艺术

ARTS IN SHENZHEN

www.szCityGuide.com

Arts in Shenzhen, an overview · 1

Shenzhen's Museums & Arts Centers · 2

Chinese Calligraphy · 3

Spring Festival through the eyes of a Child · 4

Chinese Corner · 4

Lonely Writers©

Arts in Shenzhen

Children in Shenzhen

儿童天地

CHILDREN IN SHENZHEN

www.szCityGuide.com

Children's Education · 1

Activities for Children · 2

Chinese Corner · 3

Lonely Writers©

Children in Shenzhen

Education in Shenzhen

深圳教育

EDUCATION IN SHENZHEN

www.szCityGuide.com

Learning Chinese in Shenzhen · 1

Studying Chinese at the University of Shenzhen · 2

Getting an International Education · 3

Chinese Corner · 4

Education in Shenzhen

Health in Shenzhen

深圳医疗

HEALTH IN SHENZHEN

www.szCityGuide.com

Basic health information in Shenzhen and China · 1

Recommended Hospitals in Shenzhen · 2

Recommended Densits in Shenzhen · 3

Chinese Corner · 4

Lonely Writers©

Health in Shenzhen

Modern Shenzhen and its rediscovered past

深 圳

△ 深圳, 'deep drains'
隶书 Calligraphy by 張平生
Shenzhen, March '06

Settling down in Shenzhen

Buying a property in China - 1
Importing your personal effect into Shenzhen - 2
Bringing you pet in China - 4

Chinese Corner - 4

Living in Shekou

An overview of Shekou - 1
Shekou, Seaword, and Old Shekou maps - 2
Settling down in Shekou, all you need to know - 3
Shekou's 50 best living and shopping places - 4

Chinese Corner - 5

Shekou Credits H-K

Sports Associations in Shenzhen

Traveling in Shenzhen

Getting in Shenzhen - 1
Traveling from Shenzhen - 2
Traveling Shenzhen by bus - 3
Traveling Shenzhen by MTR - 4
Chinese Corner - 5

深圳交通

TRAVELING IN SHENZHEN

www.szCityGuide.com

Lonely Writers©

Traveling in Shenzhen

Useful Information

Getting a Chinese Visa - 1
Associations in Shenzhen - 2
Banks - 3
Mobile phone & Telephone - 4
Internet Access - 5
Utilities - 6
Post Offices - 7
Useful Telephone Numbers - 8
Chinese Corner - 9

实用信息

USEFUL INFORMATION

www.szCityGuide.com

Lonely Writers©

Useful Information

And more...

Acknowledgments

- Tracy Chen 陈敏华
- Amber Qiu 邱鸿雁
- Andy Lau 劉鼎新
- Clarisse Lau
- Dave Towey
- David Lucchese
- Erica Lai 赖颖珊
- Franca Lucchese
- Heather Letterman
- Isabelle Friedrich
- James Baquet
- Justin 柳经纬
- Lison 林琛
- Mario Lucchese
- Mary Ann MacCartney
- Maryline Lucchese
- Michelle Liu 刘敏霞
- Newman C.J. Huo 霍成举
- Raffaele Lucchese
- Ranajit Dam
- Rita Liu 刘艳明
- Roger Lin 林敏
- Sara Xie 谢风
- Shierley Koval
- Soo Yee Virasith 张淑仪
- Valerie Nomain

- Vicki Steven
- Wei Hongxing 韦洪兴
- Wind Cheung 张峰
- Yolanda Favreau
- Yongli Philippe Hing 张永利
- Zhang Pingsheng 张平生

Established on July 1, 1997, Shenzhen Daily is one of the three major English daily newspapers on China's mainland as well as the sole English daily newspaper in South China. It is available every day from Monday to Friday with 16 pages per issue, covering politics, business, sports, society, culture, travel, entertainment and leisure, with authentic English, original information and unique and global perspective. Shenzhen Daily is the primary source of information for the 100,000 expatriates who permanently reside in the Pearl Delta area, providing them with exclusive and refreshing information about the mainland and Shenzhen. Shenzhen Daily also targets corporate executives, white-collar workers, public servants, and returned overseas Chinese.

students. It serves as a "living text" for English learners and as the first NIE newspaper in China it is particularly popular among middle school teachers and students. Shenzhen Daily is also one of the primary sources of information about the Pearl Delta area for the expatriates living in Hong Kong, available in more than 30 Hong Kong upscale hotels. Shenzhen Daily is the most-quoted English media in South China. It is one of the primary sources of information for almost all mainland English media. Most of the stories are cited or reprinted in Xinhuanet, gov.cn and southcn.com, to name just a few. Its official website (www.szdaily.com, www.sznews.com) launched the first digital newspaper in China in 2007 with a daily number of visitors hitting 150,000.

Frequency of publication	Monday through Friday 50 weeks per year	
Subscription	1 month: 20 yuan	3 months: 60 yuan
	6 months: 120 yuan	1 year: 240 yuan
	Call +86 755 8351 9911	
Advertising	Call +86 755 8351 9456	
Website	www.szdaily.com (English) www.sznews.com (Chinese)	
Email	szdaily@szszd.com.cn	

深圳日报
Shenzhen Daily
The only English daily on the southern Chinese mainland

责任编辑：王　淼

封面设计：朱古力设计公司

图书在版编目（CIP）数据

深圳城市物候表：英文 / 深圳日报等编. —深圳：深圳报业集团出版社，
2008.6

ISBN 978-7-80709-198-1

I. 深… II. 深… III. 座谈栏目—深圳市—英文
IV. K928.965.3

中国版本图书馆 CIP 数据核字（2008）第 089205 号

深圳城市物候表

深圳日报　编辑

深圳报业集团出版社出版发行
（518000 深圳市深南大道 6008 号）
深圳市彩帝印刷有限公司印刷　新华书店经销
2008 年 6 月第 1 版　2008 年 6 月第 1 次印刷
开本：787mm×1092mm　1/32　印张：8.5
ISBN 978-7-80709-198-1　定价：98.00 元